UNTAPPED SOURCES

*AMERICA'S
NEWSPAPER ARCHIVES
AND HISTORIES*

prepared for the
AMERICAN SOCIETY OF NEWSPAPER EDITORS'
NEWSPAPER HISTORY TASK FORCE
by the
GANNETT FOUNDATION MEDIA CENTER
AT COLUMBIA UNIVERSITY IN THE CITY OF NEW YORK
written by Jon Vanden Heuvel
edited by Craig LaMay and Martha FitzSimon

ILLUSTRATED ON COVER: *Extra!*, painting by John George Brown, from the collection of Dr. and Mrs. Kenneth Blau.

CONTENTS

FOREWORD

I recently read an account of a number of people who had lost their memories and who were therefore deprived of their very personalities and incapable of coherent action. Isn't there some comparable risk if institutions forget or neglect their histories? If they lose track of their past, aren't they somehow incapacitated in dealing with the present and the future?

The ASNE History and Newspapers Committee has determined that American newspapers will suffer no such fate—that they will quit trashing their historical artifacts and instead become mindful of their historical achievements: that they, their scholars and the public will come to a better understanding of the role the press has played in the American drama, and that they will come to see present journalistic issues in the context of what has gone before.

The history of newspapers in the United States is not always a tale of angelic creatures wrestling evil to the ground. It's a story as boisterous as the democratic adventure itself, and replete with its fair share of scoundrels. But to know the story is to celebrate the story, and along with that celebration, to understand better who and what we are. The utility of history is not the only excuse for history, but I do believe knowledge of the history of American newspapers can assist editors in coping with the troubles of the times—the challenge of the electronic media, the steady decline in household penetration of newspapers and the current drastic drop in advertising revenue, for instance.

The ASNE History and Newspapers Committee has undertaken a variety of tasks, but I am especially proud of this bibliography in narrative form.

The project would never have occurred without the cheerful assistance of Ev Dennis, executive director of the Gannett Foundation Media Center. Ev organized this undertaking, and the Center carried it out. You will find the bibliography fun to read, but please don't stop there. Read some of these books and learn more about our industry's history. I think you will enjoy yourself, and I think you will profit.

Jay Ambrose
Editor, *Rocky Mountain News*
Chairman, ASNE History and Newspapers Committee

PREFACE

IT IS SAID that newspapers lack institutional memory, and that is often true. Any close inspection of persons who make up the ownership, management and staff of any given newspaper will often reveal considerable ignorance about a given paper's history and tradition, let alone a more generalized knowledge of the history of journalism.

But American newspapers do have a rich and often well-documented history. It is a history not only unknown to many in the field of journalism, but also missing from most general American histories.

This monograph produced for the American Society of Newspapers Editors' History and Newspapers Committee by the Gannett Foundation Media Center is an effort to correct this deficiency. It not only reviews and assesses a great many books about newspapers and the people who have produced them, but also lists the major archives where journalists, scholars and citizens can go to retrieve their history.

We at the Center at Columbia University were honored to work with a committee of distinguished editors under the guidance of Jay Ambrose of the *Rocky Mountain News* in completing this work. I am particularly indebted to Jon Vanden Heuvel, my special assistant, who did most of the research and writing; to Craig LaMay and Martha FitzSimon, who caringly edited this effort; and to Penny Panoulias for her assistance.

If thoughtful ASNE members take more interest in their own rich history, perhaps even integrating it into news stories that will give local communities greater context, then this project will have been worth the effort. We hope it also proves useful to journalism historians, other scholars and citizens who believe that institutional memory is valuable.

Everette E. Dennis
Executive Director, Gannett Foundation Media Center
at Columbia University in the City of New York

INTRODUCTION

THIS REPORT focuses on what scholars increasingly recognize as a well-spring of information on American culture and history: our old newspapers. It begins with a historiographical essay on the state of scholarly research on newspapers and newspaper journalists and concludes with an inventory of the country's major newspaper collections.

The bibliographic essay is by necessity selective. A large literature exists on newspapers and newspaper journalists, and a more in-depth look at the history of American newspapering can be found in the handful of standard works narrating the story of the press in the United States. Isaiah Thomas was the first to take up newspapering as a subject for study in his book, *The History of Printing in America, with a Biography of Printers and an Account of Newspapers* (1810). Thomas' remained the classic account until editor Frederic Hudson's *Journalism in the United States from 1690 to 1872* (1873). Willard Grosvenor Bleyer's *Main Currents in the History of American Journalism* (1927) broke new ground as a scholar's accurate, organized survey, and Alfred McClung Lee's *The Daily Newspaper in America* (1937) exhibited detailed research with a sociological approach. Bleyer and Lee remain important sources for researchers, along with a 1941 classic, Frank Luther Mott's *American Journalism: A History of Newspapers,* last updated in 1962. Mott is a storehouse of newspaper data and lore stemming from meticulous research in the files. The current standard reference for newspapers and other media, Michael and Edwin Emery's *The Press and America: An Interpretive History of the Mass Media,* first appeared in 1954 and became the leading authority in the 1970s. Richard Schwarzlose's *Newspapers: A Reference Guide* (1987), to which this report is indebted, gives an exhaustive account of the literature on American newspapering. William David Sloan has also compiled an exhaustive bibliography on American journalism, *American Journalism History* (1989), which includes works on broadcasting journalism as well. Perry Ashley's three volumes on newspaper journalists in the *Dictionary of Literary Biography* is also an indispensable introduction. Among the standard bibliographies, two containing a wealth of annotations about newspapering and newspapers are Warren C. Price, *The Literature of Journalism* (1959) and Warren C. Price and Calder M. Pickett, *An Annotated Journalism Bibliography, 1958–1968* (1970).

For listings of American newspaper files, Clarence S. Brigham's *History and Bibliography of American Newspapers, 1690–1820* (1947) is a guide to surviving early newsprint (corrected and updated in 1962). Winifred Gregory's *American Newspapers, 1821–1936: A Union List of Files Available in the United States and Canada* (1936) refers to bound newsprint volumes, many of which have since been microfilmed. The Library of Congress periodically publishes *Newspapers on Microfilm,* listing holdings of cooperating libraries newspaper by newspaper. Lucy Shelton Caswell's *Guide to Sources in American Journalism History* (1989) is the most recent guide of archival and manuscript sources.

The present essay examines narrowly focused works on American newspapering rather than books on "the press" or "journalism" in general and seeks to identify gaps in the literature and point out directions for further study. The inventory of newspaper collections gives an idea of the resources available for further research. For information on collections of papers of individual journalists, scholars should consult Ashley's work and the Library of Congress' catalogue.

For the most part, information for the inventory was obtained through a questionnaire that the Gannett Center for Media Studies, now called the Gannett Foundation Media Center, sent to the nation's major newspaper repositories. The questionnaire paid particular attention to four areas: the size of the collection, the antiquity of its holdings, the subject or geographical areas in which the repositories are particularly strong, and current preservation policies and procedures.

The size of the collections, measured by the number of newspaper issues preserved, was perhaps the most difficult part of the questionnaire for the institutions to answer. Several institutions provided rough estimates of the number of issues in their collection, while others could only give a figure for the number of volumes of hard-copy newspapers (each volume containing anywhere from 10 to 100 issues) and the number of microfilm reels. Still other institutions had only the vaguest notion of the size of their collections.

Most institutions could provide a good approximation of the number of titles preserved in their collections, and this figure, along with the number of issues, is a good indicator of the breadth and diversity of the nation's various collections.

In our effort to determine the antiquity of the newspaper holdings, the Civil War provided the most convenient watershed separating colonial and early American newspapers from publications of a more recent vintage. Pre-Civil War titles are those newspapers that had a majority of issues printed before 1860. For instance, a newspaper that ran from 1840 to 1870 would be considered pre-Civil War; one that ran from 1850 to 1880 would be considered post-Civil War. The bulk of most collections was post-Civil War, the American Antiquarian Society, Library of Congress, New York Historical Society and Boston Public Library having the most significant antebellum holdings.

Predictably, the strong suit of most collections was newspapers from their own states or regions. But some institutions were thematically rather than geographically oriented. For instance, Catholic University collects Catholic newspapers on a nationwide basis, as does the Balch Institute with respect to ethnic newspapers.

Policies for preserving newspapers varied greatly among the institutions. The well endowed, such as the Library of Congress, have a systematic microfilming policy that ensures the preservation of fragile post-Civil War newspapers with high acid content. Typically, smaller institutions concentrate their microfilming efforts on local and state newspapers. Other institutions have more sporadic microfilming, depending on the availability of funding, and still others microfilm only upon patron request. All of the institutions covered in this inventory are participants in the United States Newspaper Project, sponsored by the National Endowment for the Humanities.

The U.S. Newspaper Project will be a critical source for those with well-defined research concerns who are interested in a particular title or a particular issue or issues. When completed, the Project will enable researchers to view newspapers held at different repositories around the country on a nationwide database. Although the response to our questionnaire was excellent, some institutions with considerable newspaper holdings—for example,

Yale, UCLA and the Center for Research Libraries—were unable to assess the scope or salient aspects of their holdings. While the U.S. Newspaper Project will provide scholarly researchers with a great tool, a brief overview of newspaper preservation from an institutional point of view might be of great interest to the general public, to the amateur historian, indeed to anyone with a desire to peruse a bit through our nation's past as recorded in newsprint.

RESEARCH ON NEWSPAPERS

THE ESSAY portion of this report is divided into two sections. The first examines the literature on newspapers and the second deals with books about those who produce the papers—editors, publishers and reporters. Each section gives a brief overview of the literature, listing titles and dates of publication and arranging the titles in several categories so that the vast forest of books on newspapers and journalists takes some discernible and useful shape. A handful of the most recent and representative books on newspapers and journalists is discussed at greater length. Finally, the essay closes with a few comments about directions for further study.

As the historical guild over the past three decades has turned ever more to studies of the "common man" rather than politicians and rulers, of everyday life rather than top-level diplomatic negotiations, newspapers have increased in value as sources. After the advent of the "penny press" in the 1830s, newspapers began to reach previously undreamt of masses of readers. The content of these papers is on one hand reflective of the interests, anxieties and aspirations of their broad-based readership, and on the other hand indicative of the visions and biases of their publishers, editors and reporters.

But as a subject of study itself, the newspaper presents the historian with several problems. Is the story of a newspaper essentially a story of personalities: the men and women who during the late hours in smoke-filled rooms slog through reams of reportage and battle over editorial decisions? Or can one view the newspaper as an institution with a life of its own, a great flagship tossed about by the swells of public opinion, readership, economic boom or bust, whose editors and publishers at the helm have a very limited capacity to control its course?

Until recently, the former approach has held sway. Histories of newspapers were often a litany of names and dates and firsts, and were as a rule very sympathetic to the newspaper and its purveyors. Often these books were written by staffers of the paper to celebrate a major anniversary; Thomas Ewing Dabney's *One Hundred Great Years: The Story of the Times-Picayune from Its Founding to 1940* (1944) is typical of this genre. The "in-house" quality of such histories tends to make for chatty, anecdotal writing and a rather uncritical treatment of the particular newspaper's history.

Such histories, written by non-historians, often lack a synthesizing thesis or fall into what James W. Carey criticized as a "Whig interpretation" that portrays the newspaper as steadily improving to become the paragon of journalistic excellence it was at the time of the book's writing. The greatest value in such books, perhaps, is what they reveal about the period in which they are written: what an author in 1924, for instance, likes or dislikes in surveying the preceding 100 or so years.

During the 1980s, more books appeared that emphasized the newspaper as an institution. Such studies had a more scholarly bent, examining the decision-making process within the newspaper organization, changes in readership, how these changes affected the business side of newspaper publishing, and technical innovation. Harold A. Williams' *The Baltimore Sun, 1837–1987* (1987), though commissioned for the newspaper's 150th anniversary, differs from the traditional anniversary book in its emphasis on the institutional history of the *Sun*. Chris Argyris, in his *Behind the Front Page* (1974), treats the newspaper as a "living system." In his study of the institutional structure of an anonymous newspaper he calls the *Daily Planet*, but known to be the *New York Times,* personalities are entirely left out.

Such institutional histories, like personality-dominated histories, have their own drawbacks. While they recognize the larger impersonal forces that shape a newspaper, they sometimes fail to give a flavor of what the newspaper was actually like, its journalistic style and how readers reacted to it. Ideally, the history of a newspaper should seek a balance between the personality and the individual factors that went into shaping it and the broader impersonal forces that influenced it. Such a balanced profile of the newspaper must then be placed in its specific social and historical context.

What follows is an annotated bibliography covering studies of (1) individual newspapers, (2) ethnic newspapers, (3) frontier newspapers, (4) newspapers categorized by state, city or region, (5) underground or radical newspapers and labor newspapers, (6) religious newspapers, (7) army newspapers, and (8) newspapers that are centered on specific issues that the newspaper covered.

STUDIES OF INDIVIDUAL NEWSPAPERS

ONLY GRADUALLY have newspaper historians begun to concentrate on locating the newspaper in its social context, and this is reflected by the fact that histories of individual papers far outnumber histories focusing on the ethnic, religious or political aspects of American newspapers. Most of the major metropolitan papers have had several monographs devoted to them. Howard Bray's *The Pillars of the Post: The Making of a News Empire in Washington* (1980), Tom Kelly's *The Imperial Post: The Meyers, the Grahams and the Paper That Rules Washington* (1983), and Chalmers M. Roberts' *The Washington Post: The First 100 Years* (1977) are solid studies of the *Post.* The *Los Angeles Times* is the subject of Marshall Berges' very sympathetic *The Life and Times of Los Angeles: A Newspaper, a Daily and a City* (1984), Robert Gottlieb and Irene Wolt's *Thinking Big: The Story of the Los Angeles Times, Its Publishers and Their Influence on Southern California* (1977), and Jack R. Hart's *The Information Empire: The Rise of the Los Angeles Times and the Times Mirror Corporation* (1981). Lloyd Wendt's excellent *Chicago Tribune: The Rise of a Great American Newspaper* (1979) and Philip Kinsley's now outdated *The Chicago Tribune: Its First Hundred Years* (1943) cover the *Tribune.* *The Pictured Encyclopedia of the World's Greatest Newspaper* (1928), published by the *Tribune* for its 80th anniversary, contains hundreds of photos and diagrams on newspaper production and serves as a valuable record of "hot type" production. Lloyd Wendt has also written on *The Wall Street Journal: The Story of Dow Jones and the Nation's Business Newspaper* (1982), as have Winthrop and Frances Neilson on *What's News—Dow Jones: Story of the Wall Street Journal* (1973); Jerry M. Rosenberg, *Inside the Wall Street Journal* (1982); and, most recently, Edward E. Scharff, *Worldly Power: The Making of the Wall Street Journal* (1986).

As a subject, the *New York Times* has generated a proud progeny of books, beginning with Elmer Davis' *History of the New York Times, 1851–1921*

(1921). Meyer Berger followed this with *The Story of the New York Times, 1851–1951* (1951) for the paper's 100th anniversary. Turner Catledge's *My Life and the Times* (1971) is a well-written insider's account, as is Harrison E. Salisbury's complimentary *Without Fear or Favor* (1980). Gay Talese employed the "new journalism" in his fascinating study of the *Times, The Kingdom and the Power* (1978). Ruth Adler's *A Day in the Life of the New York Times* (1981) is good on the nuts and bolts of putting out a national daily on any given day. Jane T. Harrigan's *Read All About It!* (1987) is a similar effort for the *Boston Globe*. Given its reputation as America's premier newspaper, the *Times* has of course attracted criticism as well as accolades. Herman H. Dinsmore's *All the News That Fits* (1969), for example, which makes a plea for more anti-Soviet reporting and accuses the *Times* of helping Fidel Castro to power, is useful only for those who wish to refresh their memories of the polemics of the Cold War.

Peter Pritchard's *The Making of McPaper: The Inside Story of USA Today* (1987) is a fascinating study emphasizing the entrepreneurial aspects of starting up the paper rather than scrutinizing its "journalism of hope." Pritchard had access to all the files and offers a frank treatment of *USA Today*'s successes and pitfalls. Although this essay avoids discussing books on "the press" in general, Ellis Cose's *The Press* (1989) must be mentioned. It deals with the *Washington Post*, the Times Mirror Company, the *New York Times* and the two large groups, Gannett and Knight-Ridder. Cose bases his study on extensive interviews, and successfully illustrates the intermeshing of personalities and institutions. David Halberstam's *The Powers That Be* (1979) is broader in conception, deals with non-print media as well as newspapers, but offers some interesting insights on the *Los Angeles Times*, the *Washington Post* and the *New York Times*.

Early American newspapers have received much less attention than their 20th-century descendants. William Ames' *A History of the National Intelligencer* (1972) is a first-rate study. Hennig Cohen's *The South Carolina Gazette, 1732–1775* (1953), Robert Neal Elliot Jr.'s *The Raleigh Register, 1799–1863* (1955), Jarvis Means Morse's *Connecticut Newspapers in the Eighteenth Century* (1935), Joseph Towne Wheeler's *The Maryland Press, 1777–1790* (1938) and Lawrence C. Wroth's *A History of Printing in Colonial Maryland* (1922) are others in the handful of books on 18th-century newspapering. *The Hartford Courant*, arguably America's oldest still-publishing newspaper, is the subject of John Bard McNulty's *Older Than the Nation: The Story of the Hartford Courant* (1964) and J. Eugene Smith's *One Hundred Years of Hartford's Courant, from Colonial Times Through the Civil War* (1949). Though there are few works on specific early American newspapers, the 18th-century press is naturally discussed in works about some of the nation's great early publishers, or printers as they often called themselves, Alexander Hamilton and Benjamin Franklin to name but two.

Garrett D. Byrnes and Charles H. Spilman's *The Providence Journal, 150 Years* (1980), published by the Providence Journal Company, shows that given a generous budget, histories of individual newspapers can be successful. Their book is handsomely published, full of illustrations and pictures, rich in anecdote. Other recent monographs on individual newspapers include Frank Angelo's *On Guard: A History of the Detroit Free Press* (1981), Thomas Harrison Baker's *The Memphis Commercial Appeal: The History of a Southern Newspaper* (1971), Earl L. Bell and Kenneth C. Crabbe's *The Augusta Chronicle: Indomitable Voice of Dixie, 1785–1960* (1960), Erwin D. Canham's *Commitment to Freedom: The Story of the Christian Science Monitor* (1958), John Chapman's *Tell it to Sweeney: The Informal History of the New York Daily News* (1981), Jack Claiborne's *The Charlotte Observer, Its Time and Place, 1869–1986* (1986), Lester Cohen's *The New York Graphic, The World's Zaniest Newspaper* (1964), Will C. Conrad, Kathleen F. Wilson and Dale Wilson's *The Milwaukee Journal: The First Eighty Years* (1964), Robert Neal Elliot Jr.'s *The Raleigh Register, 1799–1863* (1955), John M. Harrison's *The Blade of Toledo* (1985), Jim Allen Hart's *A History of the St. Louis Globe-Democrat* (1961), Bill Hosokawa's *Thunder in the Rockies: The Incredible Denver Post* (1976), Louis M. Lyons' *Newspaper Story: One Hundred Years of the Boston Globe* (1971), Kevin M. McAuliffe's *The Great American Newspaper: The Rise and Fall of the Village Voice* (1978), O. N. Malmquist's *The First 100 Years: A History of the Salt Lake Tribune, 1871–1971* (1971), Bradley L. Morrison's *Sunlight on Your Doorstep: The Minneapolis Tribune's First Hundred Years, 1867–1967* (1967), Donald J. O'Grady's *History at Your Door: The Story of the St. Paul Dispatch and Pioneer Press, 1849–1983* (1983), Robert L. Perkin's *The First Hundred Years: An Informal History of Denver and the Rocky Mountain News* (1959), Warren C. Price's *The Eugene Register-Guard: A Citizen of Its Community*

(1976), Julian S. Rammelkamp's *Pulitzer's Post-Dispatch, 1878–1883* (1967), Margaret Ross' *Arkansan Gazette, The Early Years, 1819–1866: A History* (1969), Joseph Sage's *Three to Zero: The Story of the Birth and Death of the World Journal Tribune* (1967), Raymond A. Schroth's *The Eagle and Brooklyn: A Community Newspaper, 1841–1955* (1974), Nixon Smiley's *Knights of the Fourth Estate: The Story of the Miami Herald* (1974), Andy Van Meter's *Always My Friend: A History of the State Journal-Register and Springfield* (1981), and John Wilds' *Afternoon Story: A Century of the New Orleans States-Item* (1976).

Regrettably, many of these histories of individual newspapers are very dry reading. In essence, the study of a single newspaper is an endeavor in micro-history—the researcher's lens is closely focused on a small subject and he or she can hence examine it in all its detail. This is both the virtue and the vice of many of these books: They contain a vast amount of detail, making them useful to the local historian or as secondary sources, but also making them rather tedious for the general reader. That is not to say that there is no need for studies of single newspapers. But unless the newspaper by virtue of its size and importance merits a study, or unless the historian is able to uncover in the history of a single newspaper a certain paradigmatic quality that would shed light on the American press in general, it is hard to see how studies of individual newspapers will ever be of interest to the broad reading public. A more fruitful direction of research probably lies in studies of newspapers organized along a thematic principle, examples of which will be discussed later.

One example of a very successful work on a single newspaper is Richard Kluger's *The Paper: The Life and Death of The New York Herald Tribune* (1986). Few would dispute that a paper having at one time or another owners such as Horace Greeley, James Gordon Bennett, John Hay Whitney or the Reids, and writers and editors such as Walter Lippmann, Jacob Riis, Henry James, Dorothy Thompson, Franklin Pierce Adams, Joseph Alsop, Charles Anderson Dana, Lucius Beebe, Red Smith, Heywood Broun and various other big names, merits a historical monograph. The previous work on "the Paper" was Royal Cortissoz's *The New York Herald Tribune: Incidents and Personalities in Its History* (1923). In addition, Kluger manages to weave several themes through his story that give the massive (801 pages) book coherence and raise broader issues of relevance to the entire American press.

Though the book covers the entire history of the *Tribune*, Kluger's main fascination is with the paper during the 20th century, its "golden age" from the late 1920s to 1947 and its subsequent decades of decline and death. Kluger presents *The Paper* as a case study in the fall of a great metropolitan daily and in so doing raises a number of other general questions, such as the value of corporate rather than family ownership of a newspaper. But while Kluger shows an understanding of the institutional mechanisms at work in *The Paper*, it is always individuals who occupy center stage, at times beneficiaries of the impersonal historical forces, at times victims of them. For instance, the paper's last owner, John Hay Whitney, emerges as a slightly culpable victim. Confronted with a declining readership due to broad shifts in the market, Whitney pumped his own fortune into keeping the *Herald Tribune* alive rather than attempting a bold repositioning of the paper in the market, and was ultimately overcome by forces greater than his own fortune. Kluger's book, then, attains that necessary balance between institutions and broad trends on the one hand, and personalities and individual decisions on the other. All this is deftly placed in its wider historical context—the pioneering years of the penny press, New York's cultural flourishing during the 1930s and 1940s, and the crippling strike in 1965 that sealed the *Tribune's* fate. *The Paper* ought to stand as a model for future works on single newspapers.

ETHNIC NEWSPAPERS

ETHNICITY is one obvious theme in American history and in the American press that would lend coherence to a study of a group of newspapers. Robert E. Park's *The Immigrant Press and Its Control* (1922) and Sally M. Miller's (ed.) *The Ethnic Press in the United States* (1987) serve as good starting points for research into this field. Lubomyr and Anna Wynar's *Encyclopedic Dictionary of Ethnic Newspapers and Periodicals* (1976)is also useful as a reference work. Miller's book, which contains 28 articles by historians, sociologists and cultural anthropologists on newspapers of different ethnic groups, is the most stimulating of the three and advances a new approach to studies of ethnic newspapers. The researcher, she suggests, must consider the ethnic newspaper to have a dual and, in a sense, contradictory role: It at once seeks to facilitate assimilation into American society and culture and to help preserve the special ethnic identity.

Surprisingly few monographs exist on the press of individual ethnic groups. The Scandinavian press is examined in William Aglow Anderson's *The Immigrant Takes His Stand: The Norwegian-American Press and Public Affairs, 1847–1852* (1953), Jonas Oscar Backhand's *A Century of the Swedish American Press* (1952), Finns Herbert Caps' *From Isolationism to Involvement: The Swedish Immigrant Press in America, 1915–1945* (1966), and Marion Marzolf's *The Danish-Language Press in America* (1979). German immigrants, particularly those liberals who immigrated after the failed 1848 revolution, operated a very high-quality press in America, especially in Midwestern states such as Illinois, Missouri, Wisconsin and Minnesota. Much work in this area remains to be done, particularly an investigation of the German press's links to the embryonic labor movement in the United States. Karl Arndt and May Olson's *German-American Newspapers and Periodicals, 1732–1955* (1961) is a comprehensive annotated bibliography that should serve as a good starting point for studies in this area. Carl Wittke's admirable but dated *The German-Language Press in America* (1957) is still the best general work on this subject. Steven Cowan's *Germans for a Free Missouri: Translations from the St. Louis Radical Press, 1857–1862* (1983) contains selections from the nine German-language newspapers published in St. Louis during the mid-19th century. Dick Hoeder's *The Immigrant Labor Press in North America, 1840–1970* (1971), an exhaustive three-volume work on the labor press of all ethnic groups, is more useful as a catalogue than as an analysis. Edmund G. Olszyk's *The Polish Press in America* (1940), Hendrick Edelman's *The Dutch-Language Press in America* (1986), and William Leonard Joyce's *Editors and Ethnicity, A History of the Irish-American Press, 1848–1883* (1976) are other works on ethnic newspapers.

The Jewish press in America lacks a standard history. Mordecai Solutes' *The Yiddish Press: An Americanizing Agency* (1925) is a solid work but is dated and does not address the more recent view of the dual role of the ethnic press that Miller's book raises. Marc D. Angel's *La America: The Sephardic Experience in the United States* (1980) is a good treatment of one particular Jewish group as reflected in its press. The American Indian press, long neglected, has more recently been the subject of scholarly research. James E. Murphy and Sharon M. Murphy's *Let My People Know: American Indian*

Journalism, 1828–1978 (1981) is a fine first study in this field. In addition, James Danny and Maureen Heady of the Wisconsin State Historical Society, where a large portion of American Indian newspapers are housed, have recently produced an excellent bibliographical guide, *Native American Periodicals and Newspapers from 1828 to 1982* (1984), which will be an invaluable aid to further research on this topic.

There is a relatively large literature on the black press in America, although a standard, all-encompassing work on the black press remains to be written. Roland E. Wolseley's *The Black Press, U.S.A.* (1971) is probably the most comprehensive work. A second, and much updated, edition of Wolseley's book appeared in 1990. Lawrence D. Hogan's recent *A Black National News Service: The Associated Negro Press and Claude Burnett, 1919–1945* (1984) is a very good study. Henry Lewis Sung's (ed.) book on *The Black Press in the South, 1865–1979* (1983) provides useful samples of black journalism but lacks a unifying thesis to tie its samples together. Some good works exist on black journalists, such as Frederick Douglass and P. D. Young, and are discussed in the next section. Other works on the black press include Carter R. Bryan's *Negro Journalism in America Before Emancipation* (1969), Martin E. Ann's (ed.) *The Black Press, 1827–1890: The Quest for National Identity* (1971), Frederick Detweiler's *The Negro Press in the United States* (1922), Lee Finkel's *Forum for Protest: The Black Press During World War II* (1976), Vishnu V. Oak's *The Negro Newspaper* (1948), and James S. Tinney and Justine J. Rector's (eds.) *Issues and Trends in Afro-American Journalism* (1980). I. Garland Penn's *The Afro-American Press and Its Editors*, first published in 1891, remains a fascinating work. The first part of the book deals with black newspapers; the second part consists of sketches of black editors and correspondents. Most of the material for this study is located at the New York Public Library's Schomburg Collection (see p. 59).

A great deal of work remains to be done on the ethnic press. Certain groups of immigrants—Italians, Chinese and hispanics, to name but three—have been neglected. Although the ethnic press saw its greatest flowering in the late-19th century, during the period of massive immigrant influx from Central and Eastern Europe, no solid monograph exists that examines the Slavic press or East European press founded by these immigrants. In addition to studies of hitherto overlooked ethnic groups, new research on the ethnic press should take into careful consideration the different political sentiments reflected in different ethnic presses. One might undertake comparative studies of different ethnic presses. How, for instance, did the German labor press differ politically from that of the Czechs or the hispanics? What differences are apparent in readership, ownership structure, and so forth? Of course, it would be facile to regard each ethnic press as somehow monolithic; one could investigate the divergent and conflicting political stances (or lack thereof) within the press of a particular ethnic group. Also one could focus on evolution and changes within the press of various ethnic groups: for instance, the crossover (or, again, lack thereof) from a foreign-language ethnic press to an English-language ethnic press. Bibliographic control and the preservation of ethnic newspapers have come a long way in recent years (see, for instance, the Balch Institute, p. 68), and further scholarly work in this field should yield most fruitful results.

FRONTIER NEWSPAPERS

THE FIELD of frontier newspapers has produced some very good studies. Frontier newspapers are exclusively a 19th-century phenomenon. Before 1800 there was virtually no press west of the original 13 states, and by 1900 the West was tamed to such an extent that it could no longer fairly be called "frontier." This section deals with books whose authors have stressed the specific and unique nature of newspaper publishing on the western frontier. Of course, many works on individual newspapers cited above touch on the particular quandaries of trying to sell newspapers to pioneers, and many works cited below in the section on newspapers by state examine frontier newspapers—for example, a Nevada newspaper from 1864 is by its very nature a frontier newspaper. The works discussed in this section, then, differ in emphasis in that their primary focus is *frontier* newspapering, and the individual paper, rather than being the centerpiece of the study, serves a more illustrative role.

Frontier newspapers were initially papers founded west of the Alleghenies and Appalachians in the first decades of the 19th century, such as the *Pittsburgh Post Gazette*. Later papers had to be printed west of the

Mississippi to qualify as frontier newspapers. Bridging the East and West of our young country, the function of these frontier newspapers was something akin to that of the railroad. Editors saw themselves as crusaders spreading knowledge and civilization into newly settled land. The presence of a newspaper in the new towns on the Western frontier symbolized the permanence of a community. Not only the news from the East provided by the paper, but the very existence of the paper was an important psychological security blanket for the settlers. Of course, these frontier newspapers suffered astonishingly high mortality rates and a huge number of them have been forever lost to historians. But many can still be found at the state historical societies in Western states and at the major repositories.

Perhaps the best studies of frontier newspapers have been studies of the press in single frontier states. George S. Hage's *Newspapers on the Minnesota Frontier, 1849–1860* (1967) is a quality book, as is Porter Stratton's 1969 work, *The Territorial Press of New Mexico.* Marilyn McAdams Sibley's *Lone Stars and State Gazettes: Texas Newspapers Before the Civil War* (1985) is encyclopedic in its collection of facts about the 400-plus newspapers in Texas from 1813 to 1860 but fails to develop a central thesis that would cast a more cohesive picture of the Texas press. William H. Lyon's *The Pioneer Editor in Missouri, 1808–1860* (1965) is a first-rate study that brings to light differing views of the frontier editor. Traditionally, the frontier editor has been viewed as a champion of civility and social change, an individualist and a community leader who left his indelible mark on the frontier town. Lyon attacks this image of the frontier editor in his work on Missouri, stressing the limits on the frontier editor—the bigoted and intolerant readership, the editor's own often deficient business acumen, and broader economic trends and settlement patterns against which the frontier editor, however rugged, was powerless. Probably in years to come historians will seek some sort of middle ground between the traditional view of the frontier editor as a relatively autonomous individual and Lyon's revision, which places him at the mercy of impersonal historical forces.

David Fridthof Halas' recent book *Boom Town Newspapers, Journalism on the Rocky Mountain Mining Frontier, 1859–1881* (1981) also focuses on editors and their attempts to bring news to isolated mountain communities. These editors tenaciously produced papers under the most primitive conditions. They vehemently guarded their turf and their readerships, and attacked rival newspapers with a stridency that makes 20th-century "newspaper wars" seem like courtly exchanges. Legh Freeman, a rapscallion editor and publisher who traveled the West with a portable press in order to avoid the wrath of his many enemies and the besmirched victims of his scurrilous stories, is the subject of two entertaining books: Thomas H. Heutermann's *Moveable Type: Biography of Legh R. Freeman* (1979) and Elizabeth Wright's less scholarly *Independence in All Things, Neutrality in Nothing: The Story of a Pioneer Journalist of the American West* (1973).

Other notable books on the frontier press include Wendell J. Ashton's work on the *Salt Lake City Deseret News, Voice in the West: Biography of a Frontier Newspaper* (1950), John Middaugh's *Frontier Newspaper: The El Paso Times* (1958), Robert F. Karlovitz's *Newspapering in the Old West: A Pictorial History of Journalism and Printing on the Frontier* (1965), and Oliver Knight's *Following the Indian Wars: The Story of the Newspaper Correspondents Among the Indian Campaigners* (1961). More titles can be found in William E. Huntzicker's historiographical essay in the first 1988 issue of *American Journalism.* It is hoped that future historians working on the frontier press will turn to more thematic approaches. One could study, for instance, the attitudes of frontier editors toward urbanization, toward the Indians, toward the notion of manifest destiny. The Spanish-language press in the Old West is another neglected topic.

NEWSPAPERS BY STATE, CITY AND REGION

GEOGRAPHIC CRITERIA can be used to identify a group of newspapers for study. Thus far, scholars have tended to conduct studies of newspapers in a given state more than they have of newspapers in a given city or newspapers in a given region. This is unfortunate, because a state is in a sense a more artificial geographic entity than a city or region. The state often exists foremost as a legal entity, whereas cities or regions have a deeper cultural, social and economic identity. In terms of newspapers, this means that a small-town paper in upstate New York has more in common with its counterpart in Vermont than with the New York *Daily News.* Thus a history of

New York City newspapers or a study of small-town papers in America's Northeast might be more useful topics than a history of newspapers in New York state. Perhaps the fact that state historical societies often serve as both preservationist of old newspapers and as sponsor (along with state press organizations) of studies accounts for the numerical superiority of histories of newspapers by state to histories of newspapers by city or region.

Books on newspapers of a given state often combine historical narrative with a bibliographic guide. They tend to be more useful as secondary sources than interesting as general reading in and of themselves. Some titles include Fred W. Allsopp, *History of the Arkansas Press for a Hundred Years and More* (1922); Cecil J. Alter, *Early Utah Journalism: A Half Century of Forensic Warfare Waged by the West's Most Militant Press* (1938); Warren J. Brier and Nathan Blumberg, *A Century of Montana Journalism* (1971); Sam Gilhily, *The Press Gang: A Century of Montana Newspapers, 1885–1985* (1986); Louis Turner Griffith and John Erwin Talmadge, *Georgia Journalism, 1763–1950* (1957); Lola Homsher, *Guide to Wyoming Newspapers, 1867–1967* (1971); Robert F. Karlovitz, *With a Shirt Tail Full of Type: The Story of Newspapering in South Dakota* (1982); Richard E. Lingenfelter and Karen Rix Gash, *The Newspapers of Nevada: A History and Bibliography, 1854–1979* (1984); Alan Robert Miller, *The History of Maine Newspapers* (1978); Donald E. Oehlerts, *Guide to Wisconsin Newspapers, 1833–1957* (1958); William Taft, *Missouri Newspapers* (1964); and George S. Turnbull, *History of Oregon Newspapers* (1939). By limiting the time frame of their studies of state newspapers, some authors have sacrificed the broad overview for a more narrowly focused study with deeper analysis. Millard B. Grimes' *The Last Linotype: The Story of Georgia and Its Newspapers Since World War II* (1985) (weighing in at 673 pages!); Edward C. Kemble's *A History of California Newspapers 1846–1858* (1962); James B. Merriwether's *South Carolina Journals and Journalists* (1975), which concentrates on the mid-19th century; Douglas C. McMurtrie and Albert H. Allen's *Early Printing in Colorado* (1935); or the Wisconsin State Historical Society's *Wisconsin Newspapers, 1833–1850* (1958); along with the books mentioned above by Jarvis Means Morse, Joseph Towne Wheeler, Lawrence C. Wroth (see p. 4) and Marilyn McAdams Sibley, Porter Stratton and George S. Hage (see p. 11), exemplify this trend in research.

Studies of newspapers in a single city have not been sufficiently pursued. The best work of this type is probably John J. McPhaul's *Deadlines and Monkeyshines: The Fabled World of Chicago Journalism* (1962). John Bruce's *Gaudy Century: The Story of San Francisco's Hundred Years of Robust Journalism* (1948), Lenoir Chambers and Joseph C. Shrank's *Salt Water and Printer's Ink: Norfolk and Its Newspapers, 1865–1965* (1967), Louis W. Doll's *A History of Newspapers of Ann Arbor, 1829–1920* (1958), and William L. King's *The Newspaper Press of Charleston, S.C.* (1872) are other studies of newspapers by city. David Sachsman and Warren Sloat's *The Press and the Suburbs, The Daily Newspapers of New Jersey* (1985) is an excellent analytical study on the interaction of small-town local papers and the nearby big metropolitan dailies.

It is hardly worth mentioning that there are many important cities where newspaper studies could be undertaken. It would be interesting, for example, to investigate the relationship between politics in a city and competition among the city's papers. To what extent were newspapers made into mouthpieces for the political factions in the city, to what degree did city officials try to repress an acrid oppositional press, to what degree did newspapers adjust their politics to suit the tastes of their readers, and how in turn would such a shift in the political slant of a leading newspaper alter the political complexion of a city? The entanglement and interaction of a city's politics and its press are complex subjects and, in the proper hands, could make for a fascinating study. An excellent example of this multidisciplinary approach is David Paul Nord's *Newspapers and New Politics, Midwestern Municipal Reform, 1890–1900* (1981). Here Nord analyzes the major dailies in Chicago and St. Louis and shows how they helped to create a common political reality for the citizens of those cities, and by extension, how they shaped municipal reform.

Books on newspapers by region are few and far between. Of course, books on colonial newspapers are by definition about newspapers from the East Coast region. Studies of frontier newspapers are also in a sense regional studies. In addition, personal memoirs and biographies of newspapermen and newspaperwomen often offer insights into the nature of a particular region. Hodding Carter's books on the Southern press, which are discussed later, are excellent examples of this. Books on regionally based newspaper chains, such as *The Lee Papers: A Saga of Midwestern Journalism* (1947), produced by the Lee organization, also take a regional view to newspapering. William L. Rivers and David M. Rubin's *A Region's Press: Anatomy of Newspapers in the San Francisco Bay Area* (1971) is also a worthwhile regional study. One interesting recent publication that defies quick categorization is Dickson J. Preston's *Newspapers of Maryland's Eastern Shore* (1987). Maryland's eastern shore may not be the most obvious region to study, but Preston lived there, is intimately familiar with the area's past, and persuasively portrays it not only as a geographic unity but also as a social unity. Preston's keen focus on local editors and publishers and sensitive treatment of local political traits and social norms makes this a first-rate book that should serve as a model for future regional newspaper studies.

Much interesting work could be done on major themes in American history from the viewpoint of regional presses. One could investigate, for instance, American isolationism by the attitudes of regional presses—the Midwestern press, the New England press, or the press of the Old South during the era of the two world wars. Do regional differences in attitudes toward intervention in Europe emerge? If so, to what can these differences be attributed? To the education or the amount of contact with Europe that newspapermen and newspaperwomen and readers from a particular region had? To the ethnic background of editors and publishers? To deep-seated regional political traditions? Another approach would be to examine newspapers from an economically rooted regional entity—a study of newspapers from the steel belt, or a study of newspapers from the oil-producing states, for instance. Do we find in examining the papers that a common political attitude has taken shape, reflecting common economic interests? Studies of newspapers on a regional basis certainly present the researcher with a wide field of unexplored possibilities.

UNDERGROUND, ALTERNATIVE AND RADICAL NEWSPAPERS

ALTHOUGH these three types of newspapers are conveniently grouped together, underground, alternative and radical newspapers are not necessarily synonymous. Underground newspapers, as the name suggests, are never really intended for consumption by the wider public. Indeed, their very purpose is to challenge the dominant culture, politically or in terms of lifestyle. The term underground is usually applied to papers published in the 1960s and early 1970s such as New York's *Rat* or *The Berkeley Tribe*. Alternative is a term often used interchangeably with underground, but can be said to imply a less strident countercultural stance than underground newspapers and is less strictly associated with the '60s. *The Village Voice* might fall under the category alternative. "Radical" is a term stemming from 19th-century leftist political movements. It can be applied to left-wing papers of the 1960s, but, having an older pedigree, the "radical press" also refers to the socialist and anarchist press of the 19th century and the Communist press of the 20th century.

Lauren Kessler's *The Dissident Press: Alternative Journalism in American History* (1984) is the best starting place for someone interested in this subject. Kessler provides a good general overview of black, feminist, immigrant, socialist, communist, anarchist, utopian and pacifist newspapers. David Armstrong's *A Trumpet to Arms: Alternative Media in America* (1981) is also a good introduction, though not strictly confined to newspapers.

The flourish of underground newspapers a couple of decades ago has attracted the interest of a number of writers. These newspapers tended to have very local circulations, and sometimes concentrated on a single issue— the Vietnam War, black empowerment, the back-to-nature lifestyle, the use of mind-altering drugs. Robert J. Glessing's *The Underground Press in America* (1970), Everette E. Dennis' *The Magic Writing Machine* (1971), Lawrence Leamer's *The Paper Revolutionaries: The Rise of the Underground Press* (1972), Roger Lewis' *Outlaws of America* (1972), and Everette E. Dennis and William L. Rivers' *Other Voices: The New Journalism in America* (1974) are early works on the underground newspapers. Abe Peck's fascinating 1985 study, *Uncovering the Sixties: The Life and Times of the Underground Press*, benefits from a dozen years of perspective on the underground press during its heyday, 1964–1973. Peck is sensitive to variations in the underground press from city to city and region to region, and offers a fair assessment of its failings and accomplishments. Jeffrey Rips, in *The Campaign Against the Underground Press* (1981), has examined the FBI's attempts to harass, surveil and smother the underground press in the 1960s and 1970s.

More work needs to be done on the more strictly political radical press antedating the 1960s. During the late-19th and early-20th centuries, social-ism, anarchism and syndicalism had their adherents in the United States, though on a vastly smaller scale than in Europe. The radical journalism of many of these movements died out in the 1940s and 1950s and was reincar-nated in the 1960s, but in an entirely different form in which the exuberance of a youthful subculture often took the place of the more academic political discussion of the radical papers at the turn of the century.

Joseph R. Conlin's (ed.) *The American Radical Press, 1880–1960* (1974) is a good introduction to the older generation of radical press. Elliot Shore's recent *Talkin' Socialism, J. A. Wayland and the Role of the Press in American Radicalism, 1890–1912* (1988) is an excellent study of the *Appeal to Reason*, America's best-selling socialist newspaper, a weekly from Girard, Kansas. Its publisher, J. A. Wayland, emerges as an engaging contradiction in terms: a wealthy entrepreneur who preached a socialist creed in a paper run with as much concern for the bottom line as any capitalist newspaper. This points to a common thread in American radical journalism that could make for an interesting study: its ambiguous attitude toward the commercial aspects of running a newspaper. Radical newspapers, both of the 1890s and the 1960s, explicitly or implicitly rejected the capitalist/materialist mode of life in the United States. Just how the radical newspapers met costs, handled advertising and dealt with profits could make for a worthwhile study bridging both peri-ods. Two good bibliographical works on the radical press are *Radical Periodicals in the United States*, published by Greenwood Press, and *Undergrounds: A Union List of Alternative Periodicals* (1974), published by the Wisconsin State Historical Society.

Labor newspapers do not exactly fit under this category, since they were mostly union-oriented and more interested in ameliorating the condition of the working class than in a radical overthrow of the system. The research in this area has been inadequate. Some good studies of individual papers exist: Morris U. Schappes' *The Daily Worker: Heir to the Great Tradition* (1944), David Corbin's *The Socialist and Labor Star* (1951), and Elmer A. Beck's *Autopsy of a Labor Daily, The Milwaukee Leader* (1970). In addition, there is Steven Rowan's selection of clips from the German press in Missouri. No comprehensive work on the American labor press has been written.

RELIGIOUS NEWSPAPERS

THE RELIGIOUS ASPECTS of American newspapering comprise a wide-open field. In the West and the South during the 19th century, newspapers were often founded with an expressly religious point of view. In many cases new communities were established by religious congregations moving westward, perhaps led by their pastor, in search of better opportunities, more freedom and a purity of lifestyle. Their newspapers reflected the religious character of their communities. Similarly, throughout the country, newspapers of homogeneous ethnic communities might reflect the confessional makeup of the community, the prominent priest or minister or rabbi often wielding considerable influence with the local newspaper. Martin Marty's *The Religious Press in America* (1963) would serve as the best introduction to the topic generally, but focuses more on magazines than on newspapers. Paul J. Foik's *Pioneer Catholic Journalism* (1930) is an early endeavor in this field. More recently, Monte Burr McLaws' *Spokesman for the Kingdom: Early Mormon Journalism and the Deseret News, 1830–1898* (1977) is an interesting study. Nancy Roberts' *Dorothy Day and the Catholic Worker* (1984) is a very good study—less a biography of Dorothy Day than an examination of the philosophy of the *Catholic Worker*. Apollinaris Baumgartner's *Catholic Journalism: A Study of Its History in the United States, 1789–1930* (1931) was an early attempt at synthesis.

ARMY NEWSPAPERS

ALFRED E. CORNEBISE has written two first-rate books telling the story of *The Amaroc News, The Daily Newspaper of the American Forces in Germany, 1919–1923* (1981) and *The Stars and Stripes: Doughboy Journalism in World War I* (1984). Two other books that are rich in anecdotal material are Brad Hutton and Andy Rooney's *The Story of the Stars and Stripes* (1946) and John Sharnik and Oliver Gregg Howard's *Stripes: The First Five Years of the G.I.'s Newspaper* (1949).

RESEARCH ON NEWSPAPERS

NEWSPAPER STUDIES DEALING WITH SPECIFIC ISSUES AND EVENTS

THIS IS PERHAPS THE MOST PROMISING DIRECTION for future scholars of American newspapering. Rather than focusing on individual newspapers, as have the bulk of studies of American newspapers up to now, scholars might undertake broader comparative and more analytical projects by examining how specific issues and events have been covered, interpreted and portrayed by groups of newspapers. There are a few excellent books that take this approach and can serve as models for future studies. Arthur M. Schlesinger's *Prelude to Independence: The Newspaper War on Britain, 1764–1776* (1958) and Bernard Bailyn and John B. Hench's (eds.) *The Press and the American Revolution* (1980) are stimulating and well written and should serve as good starting points for anyone interested in newspapers during the Revolutionary period. Thomas C. Leonard's innovative study, *The Power of the Press: The Birth of American Political Reporting* (1986), shows how the press provided a necessary vernacular for political discussion in the early years of the Republic. One might also turn to Robert Darton and Daniel Roche's new book on newspapers in France during the French Revolution, *Revolution in Print: The Press in France, 1775–1800* (1989) for methodological insights.

There are also some very good studies of the press and the Civil War. Foremost among these are J. Cutler Andrews' two volumes, *The North Reports the Civil War* (1955) and *The South Reports the Civil War* (1970). The Southern view of events at mid-19th century is also the subject of Hodding Carter's *Their Words Were Bullets: The Southern Press in War, Reconstruction and Peace* (1969) and Donald E. Reynolds' *Editors Make War: Southern Newspapers in the Secession Crisis* (1970). Peter Braestrup's *Big Story: How the American Press and Television Reported and Interpreted the Crisis of Tet 1968 in Vietnam and Washington* (1977) is a sophisticated study focusing on a subject sufficiently narrow to allow for in-depth analysis. Carolyn Martindale's *The White Press and Black America* (1985) looks at coverage of blacks in four of the nation's major dailies.

It is hardly surprising that journalistic coverage of wars and cataclysmic events has attracted scholarly attention. But slower-moving issues and events and their treatment by the press can also make for fruitful studies. Marvin Olasky's *The Press and Abortion, 1838–1988* (1988), Eric P. Veblen's *The Manchester Union Leader in New Hampshire Elections* (1975), and Wayne Parsons' *The Power of the Financial Press: Journalism and Economic Opinion in Britain and America* (1989), are examples of this. Loren Ghiglione addresses the issue of chain ownership in *The Buying and Selling of America's Newspapers* (1984). Michael Schudson, in *Discovering the News: A Social History of American Newspapers* (1978), and Dan Schiller, in *Objectivity and the News: The Public and the Rise of Commercial Journalism* (1981), trace the emergence of objectivity and the separation of fact and opinion as cardinal values in American newspapering. There are as many topics of this sort as one's imagination allows. One might look at how the press has portrayed the issue of taxation from the tax revolts of the 1970s to the budget deficits of the 1980s. One could examine the journalistic treatment of the penal system, of the temperance movement, of presidential campaigns. One might compare newspaper coverage of American intervention in the wars in Korea and Vietnam, or look at how newspapers in the East portrayed the West in their coverage of the California gold rush, to offer but a few possibilities.

BOOKS ABOUT JOURNALISTS

BOOKS ABOUT JOURNALISTS—editors, publishers, correspondents, essayists—far outnumber books about newspapers themselves. Biography as a genre has a much older pedigree than studies of institutions such as newspapers, and apart from very well-written studies of newspapers, biographies seem to make for more accessible reading for a wider public. Many editors, publishers and reporters had prestigious careers above and beyond their work in newspapers—Benjamin Franklin, Alexander Hamilton, William Cullen Bryant and Mark Twain, to name but a few—and thus biographies that assess their whole careers shed, or should shed, some light on their newspaper days. In addition, many journalists were fastidious keepers of diaries and memoirs, or wrote autobiographies, and these serve as valuable sources in evaluating American history and the history of newspapers in particular. Some journalists, as Richard Schwarzlose has pointed out, have acquired inflated reputations simply because of the massive written record they left behind. Also, editors and publishers, because of their power, wealth and social prestige, have overshadowed reporters and correspondents in terms of the scholarly attention they attract. There are probably more studies of Horace Greeley than there are of all 19th-century reporters combined.

This second section of the bibliographic essay will examine the literature on editors, publishers, reporters and other journalists: first, the 18th-century newspapermen, lumping editors, publishers and reporters together; then 19th-century journalists, sorting out works on editors and publishers from works on reporters-correspondents-essayists; finally, 20th-century journalists, organized in the same manner as those of the 19th century.

18TH-CENTURY JOURNALISTS

IN THE 18TH AND 19TH CENTURIES, the line dividing a career in journalism and one in politics was much less rigid than it is today. Often journalists would use their reputations as a springboard into politics and then move back into journalism with equal ease. The line between careers in literature and journalism, between religion and journalism, or law and journalism was similarly porous. Benjamin Franklin, Alexander Hamilton, Thomas Paine and William Cobbett are just four examples of men who had careers in both journalism and politics. The lines between journalism and literature, journalism and law, and journalism and religion were often equally porous. Lawrence C. Wroth's *The Colonial Printer* (1938) is probably still the best introduction to the topic. Two excellent biographies of Franklin exist: Carl Van Doren's classic *Benjamin Franklin* (1938) and Claude-Anne Lopez and Eugenia W. Herbert's *The Private Franklin: The Man and His Family* (1975). David Freeman Hawke's *Franklin* (1976) covers his career up to 1776 and thus devotes a good deal of attention to Franklin's early days as publisher of the *Pennsylvania Gazette*, among other lesser known papers. Richard E. Amacher's *Benjamin Franklin* (1962) is a solid critical introduction to Franklin as a writer. Franklin's *Autobiography* retains its fascination for 20th-century readers. The 1964 edition edited by Leonard W. Labaree is the best version of this work. Labaree has also edited Franklin's *Papers*—a task that has thus far produced 24 volumes. The first three volumes contain writings dealing with Franklin's early newspaper activity.

Alexander Hamilton's career—as military leader, as lawyer, as secretary of the treasury and as publisher of the *New York Evening Post*, which he founded in 1801—is typical of the Renaissance lives that the founding fathers led and testifies to the versatility of our nation's early newspapermen. There are a number of recent biographies of Hamilton: Jacob E. Cooke's *Alexander Hamilton* (1982), Marie B. Hecht's *Odd Destiny: The Life of Alexander Hamilton* (1982), Robert A. Hendrickson's *The Rise and Fall of Alexander Hamilton* (1981), Forrest McDonald's *Alexander Hamilton: A Biography* (1979), Holmes M. Alexander's *To Covet Honor: A Biography of Alexander*

Hamilton (1977) and Broadus Mitchell's *Alexander Hamilton: A Concise Biography* (1976).

Thomas Paine might today be viewed as more pamphleteer than newspaperman, but in the 18th century the distinction between these two was blurred. The standard biography of Paine is Moncure Daniel Conway's two-volume *The Life of Thomas Paine* (1892). More recently, Alfred Owen Aldridge's *Man of Reason: The Life of Thomas Paine* (1959) is a fine work. David Freeman Hawke's *Paine* (1974) and Jerome D. Wilson and William F. Ricketson's *Thomas Paine* (1978) are substantially devoted to analyzing Paine's literary output.

Anna Janney DeArmond's *Andrew Bradford, Colonial Journalist* (1949) sketches the life and work of the founder of the *American Weekly Mercury* in 1719. John Peter Zenger printed what was probably the first opposition newspaper in the colonies, the *New York Weekly Journal*. In those days, an oppositional press was hardly a clearly acceptable vehicle of opinion, and Zenger was arrested and tried for seditious libel. Vincent Buranelli's (ed.) *The Trial of Peter Zenger* (1957), and James Alexander's *A Brief Narrative of the Case and Trial of John Peter Zenger, Printer of the New York Weekly Journal* (1963) cover this episode and Zenger's ultimate acquittal, which has gone down in history as a landmark victory for freedom of the press in America. Zenger's career is assessed in Livingston Rutherford's *John Peter Zenger: His Press, His Trial and a Bibliography of Zenger Imprints, Also a Reprint of the First Edition of the Trial* (1907).

Hugh Gaine, founder in 1752 of the *New York Mercury*, considered by many of his contemporaries to be the best newspaper in the colonies, has gone down in history as a turncoat because of his conversion to loyalism during the British occupation of New York City in 1776. Alfred L. Lorenz examines his career in *Hugh Gaine: A Colonial Printer-Editor's Odyssey to Loyalism* (1972). William Goddard, an ambitious editor who ran newspapers in Philadelphia, Baltimore, Providence and New York City is discussed in Ward Miner's biography *William Goddard, Newspaperman* (1962). Philip Freneau, better remembered for his poetry, was also one of the most influential editors of his day, serving as editor of the *New York Daily Advertiser*, *National Gazette* and *Jersey Chronicle*. His life is described in Lewis Leary's *That Rascal Freneau: A Study in Literary Failure* (1941), Jacob Axelrad's *Philip Freneau*

(1967), Philip M. Marsh's *Philip Freneau, Poet and Journalist* (1968) and Mary Weatherspoon Bowden's *Philip Freneau* (1976). Joseph Dennie, who along with Royall Tyler wrote perhaps America's first literary and political column, "Colon and Sondee," is treated in Harold Milton Ellis' *Joseph Dennie and His Circle* (1915).

Isaiah Thomas was probably the 18th century's most important newspaperman, not only for the numerous New England newspapers he published but also for his contributions to journalism as a discipline—his books on publishing and his early history of American newspapering. Annie Russell Marble's *From Prentice to Patron: The Life Story of Isaiah Thomas* (1935) is an excellent biography. Clifford K. Shipton's more concise *Isaiah Thomas: Printer, Patriot and Philanthropist* (1948) also covers Thomas' career.

William Cobbett was an Englishman who moved to the United States in 1793 and became one of the respected voices in the Federalist camp. A prolific writer on all things political, a historian and reformer, Cobbett wrote in America as Peter Porcupine, editor of *Porcupine's Gazette and Daily Advertiser*, published in Philadelphia. Biographies of Cobbett include John W. Osborne's *William Cobbett: His Thought and His Times* (1966), G. D. H. Cole's *The Life of William Cobbett* (1924), Marjorie Bowen's *Peter Porcupine: A Study of William Cobbett, 1762–1835* (1936), James Sambrook's *William Cobbett* (1973), and Karen K. List's study *The Role of William Cobbett in Philadelphia's Party Press, 1794–1799* (1983). Cobbett's own *The Autobiography of William Cobbett: The Progress of a Plow-boy to a Seat in Parliament* (1947), edited by William Reitzel, and his letters, edited by Lewis-Saul Benjamin in 1913 and by Gerald Duff in 1974, are valuable sources.

Other works on 18th-century journalists include Charles Stille's *The Life and Times of John Dickinson, 1732–1808* (1891), John C. Miller's *Sam Adams, Pioneer in Propaganda* (1936), Richard F. Hixson's *Isaac Collins, A Quaker Printer in 18th-Century America* (1968), William E. Foster's *Stephen Hopkins, A Rhode Island Statesman* (1884), Horace E. Scudder's *Noah Webster* (1881), and J. Winston Coleman Jr.'s *John Bradford, Esq.: Pioneer Kentucky Printer and Historian* (1950).

Several important 18th-century journalists warrant more extensive biographical inquiry than they have thus far received. These include William Bradford III, John Holt, Eleazer Oswald, James Parker, William Parks and

Benjamin Towne. But a more fruitful research approach than biography might be found in examining the close interaction of journalism and politics during this period. Studies that group newspaper journalists under broad political categories—for example, "The Whig Journalists," "The Tory Journalists," "The Federalist Journalists"—would be most interesting. Also a close examination of several Whig newspapers, for instance, would throw light on just what "Whiggishness" was on a grass-roots level in the 18th century. William David Sloan's article on the early party press in *Journalism History* (1982) makes several suggestions in this direction. In the proper hands, a prosopographical study of 18th-century journalists would be a fascinating and important contribution to our understanding of American journalism. To what extent did journalists come from similar (or varied) socioeconomic backgrounds? What familial and business ties existed among the editors and publishers, and how did the political stances of their newspapers reflect their personal backgrounds? A study that closely examines the biographical essentials of a number of journalists might be able to answer some of these questions.

19TH-CENTURY EDITORS AND PUBLISHERS

THERE IS A LARGE BODY OF LITERATURE on 19th-century editors and publishers. Many of these works, mostly biographies, were written by contemporaries of their subjects and thus lack a certain historical perspective. Yet a good number of them, some more than a century old, are of high quality. The life of Thomas Ritchie, the editor and publisher of the *Richmond Enquirer* who enjoyed Thomas Jefferson's patronage and became one of the principal voices of the Democratic party, is recounted by Charles Henry Ambler in *Thomas Ritchie: A Study in Virginia Politics* (1913). David Kaser's *Joseph Charles, Printer in the Western Country* (1963) tells the story of Missouri's pioneer journalist and founder of the *St. Louis Missouri Gazette* in 1808. Hezekiah Niles, whose *Weekly Register* was perhaps the most authoritative political paper of the early 19th century, is discussed in *Hezekiah Niles as an Economist* (1933) by Richard Gabriel Stone. Samuel Bangs, Texas' first newspaperman of note, is discussed in Lota M. Spell's *Pioneer Printer: Samuel*

Bangs in Mexico and Texas (1963). John T. Flanagan's *James Hall, Literary Pioneer of the Ohio Valley* (1941), Don E. Fehrenbacher's *Chicago Giant: A Biography of "Long John" Wentworth* (1957), Mary Wheelhouse Berthel's *Horns of Thunder: The Life and Times of James M. Goodhue* (1948) and Richard B. Eide's *North Star Editor: A Brief Sketch of Joseph A. Wheelock and His Policies as Editor of the St. Paul Pioneer Press* (1944) are other biographies of founders and early editors of newspapers on the Western frontier.

Mordecai Noah was perhaps the first Jewish-American to enter into the newspaper business when he founded the *New York Enquirer* in 1826. Isaac Goldberg's *Major Noah, American-Jewish Pioneer* (1936) and Jonathan Sarna's *Jacksonian Jew: The Two Worlds of Mordecai Noah* (1980) assess the life of this early American publisher. Noah's New York publishing rival, James Watson Webb, owner of the *Morning Courier*, bought the *Enquirer* from Noah in 1829 and merged the papers to form the *Courier and Enquirer*, bringing together some of New York's best journalistic talent, including James Gordon Bennett, Noah's former associate editor. The life of the combative Webb, who fought numerous duels arising from his editorial activities, is told by James L. Crouthamel in *James Watson Webb: A Biography* (1969). Two of Webb's publishing adversaries were Gerald Hallock and David Hale, owners of the *New York Journal of Commerce*. Their careers are recounted in the *Life of Gerald Hallock: Thirty-three Years as Editor of the New York Journal of Commerce* (1869) by Hallock's son, William H. Hallock; and in *Memoir of David Hale*, written in 1850 by Joseph P. Thompson.

Like Philip Freneau in the 18th century, William Cullen Bryant and Walt Whitman were two 19th-century poets who simultaneously pursued careers in journalism—Bryant as editor of Hamilton's old *New York Evening Post* from 1826 to 1878, and Whitman in a brief stint as editor of the *Brooklyn Daily Eagle* from 1846 to 1848. Parke Godwin, an associate of Bryant's at the *Evening Post*, has written the standard *A Biography of William Cullen Bryant, with Extracts from His Private Correspondence* (2 vols., 1883). Three fine recent works on Bryant are Curtis S. Johnson's *Politics and a Belly-full: The Journalistic Career of William Cullen Bryant* (1962), Charles H. Brown's *William Cullen Bryant* (1971) and Albert F. McLean Jr.'s *William Cullen Bryant* (1964). Whitman's life story is told in Frances V. Grebanier's (also known as Frances Winwar) *American Giant: Walt Whitman and His*

Times (1941) and Emory Holloway's *Whitman: An Interpretation in Narrative* (1926); his journalistic endeavors are covered in Thomas L. Brasher's *Whitman as Editor of the Brooklyn Daily Eagle* (1970). Shelley Fisher Fishkin's interesting study *From Fact to Fiction, Journalism and Imaginative Writing in America* (1985) examines the crossover between journalism and literary careers, and has chapters on Whitman, Mark Twain, Theodore Dreiser, Ernest Hemingway and John Dos Passos.

Newspaper publishers and editors were among the leaders in the campaign to abolish slavery. Perhaps the greatest abolitionist editor was William Lloyd Garrison, whose courageous writings in *The Liberator*, which he edited and published from 1831 to 1865, piqued the nation's conscience. Garrison's children produced a four-volume study of his life in 1885. More recent books on Garrison include Russell B. Nye's *William Lloyd Garrison and the Humanitarian Reformers* (1955), Walter M. Merrill's *Against Wind and Tide: A Biography of William Lloyd Garrison* (1963) and John L. Thomas' *The Liberator: William Lloyd Garrison, a Biography* (1963). Elijah P. Lovejoy, a Presbyterian minister and abolitionist editor who was killed in 1837 while defending his press from a hostile mob, is portrayed by his brothers, Joseph C. and Owen Lovejoy, in *Memoir of the Rev. Elijah Lovejoy, Who Was Murdered in Defense of the Liberty of the Press, at Alton, Illinois, Nov. 7, 1837* (1838). John Gill's *Tide Without Turning: Elijah P. Lovejoy and Freedom of the Press* (1958) and Merton L. Dillon's *Elijah P. Lovejoy, Abolitionist Editor* (1961) are also fine studies. Cassius M. Clay, a tenacious Kentucky abolitionist, is discussed in David L. Smiley's *Lion of White Hall: The Life of Cassius M. Clay* (1962).

Frederick Douglass, as founder of *The North Star*, later renamed *Frederick Douglass' Paper*, was the most influential black journalist in the anti-slavery movement. Philip Foner's five-volume *Life and Writings of Frederick Douglass* (1950), part biography and part selections of Douglass' writing, is the most comprehensive work on Douglass. Other biographies include Anna Bontemps' *Free at Last: The Life of Frederick Douglass* (1971), Booker T. Washington's *Frederick Douglass* (1971), and Benjamin Quarles' *Frederick Douglass* (1948). I. Garland Penn's 1891 work *The Afro-American Press and Its Editors* (reprinted in 1969) contains many interesting sketches of 19th-century black newspapermen. Willis Augustus Hodges, a black abolitionist publisher, wrote his autobiography, *Free Man of Color: The Autobiography of Willis Augustus Hodges*, which was edited in 1982 by Willard B. Gatewood Jr. Beyond the borders of the United States black journalists were also crusading for the abolition of slavery, as Peter G. Ripley's (ed.) *The Black Abolitionist Papers in Canada, 1830–1865* (1987) illustrates. One of the most fascinating stories that has recently come to light is that of Jean-Charles Houzeau. Houzeau was a dark-complected Belgian nobleman who moved to New Orleans and was taken for a black man. Houzeau did nothing to dispel this misconception and went on to become editor of the French-language *Tribune de la Nouvelle-Orleans*, the city's first black newspaper. His memoirs, *My Passage at the New Orleans Tribune* (1984), provide unique insight into race relations at mid-19th century and into the opportunities for and obstacles to black newspapering.

Horace Greeley has probably received more attention than any other newspaperman of the 19th century. Greeley helped pioneer the penny press with his founding of the *New York Tribune* in 1841, and until his death in 1872 used the editorship of that paper as a pulpit to expound Whig views on virtually every public issue of his day. Of the numerous biographies of Greeley, James Parton's *The Life of Horace Greeley* (1896), Glyndon Van Deusen's *Horace Greeley: Nineteenth-century Crusader* (1953), William Harlan Hale's *Horace Greeley, Voice of the People* (1950) and Erik S. Lunde's concise *Horace Greeley* (1981) are the best. In *Horace Greeley and the Tribune in the Civil War* (1936), Ray Fahrney examines Greeley's impact upon political and military policy during the conflict. Greeley was hardly reticent when it came to writing about himself. His *Recollections of a Busy Life* is an invaluable portal into 19th-century American politics and culture.

Glyndon Van Deusen assesses the political outlook of Greeley's early mentor, the Albany publisher Thurlow Weed, in *Thurlow Weed, Wizard of the Lobby* (1947). Greeley's successor at the *Tribune*, Whitelaw Reid, who later became ambassador to France and England and an unsuccessful vice-presidential candidate, is discussed in Royal Cortissoz's two-volume *The Life of Whitelaw Reid* (1921) and in Bingham Duncan's *Whitelaw Reid, Journalist, Politician, Diplomat* (1975). Reid's own writings—on the Civil War, on Greeley, on the United States and on literature in general—provide a wealth of insights into American attitudes in the second half of the 19th century. His work as a Civil War correspondent has been collected in *A Radical View: The "Agate" Dispatches of Whitelaw Reid 1861-1865* (1976), edited by James G. Smart.

James Gordon Bennett, an underling of Noah Webster early in his career, broke with the *Courier and Enquirer* and went on to found in 1835 what became New York's most successful paper, the *New York Herald.* Isaac Pray, an associate of Bennett's, wrote the *Memoirs of James Gordon Bennett and His Times* (1855), which has a wealth of inside information. Oliver Carlson's *The Man Who Made News* (1942) is also a very good study of Bennett's career. In 1867 Bennett turned over the reins of the *Herald* to his *bon vivant* son, James Gordon Bennett Jr. Primarily remembered for his prodigal spending, Bennett did oversee some important journalistic innovations during his tenure at the paper. Albert S. Crockett's *When James Gordon Bennett Was Caliph of Baghdad* (1926) and Richard O'Connor's *The Scandalous Mr. Bennett* (1962) discuss his life. Father and son are portrayed in Don C. Seitz's *The James Gordon Bennetts* (1928).

Two important 19th-century editors whose careers have tended to be overshadowed by those of Greeley, Bryant or the Bennetts are Samuel Bowles III and Charles Anderson Dana. Both were highly respected for producing two of the nation's finest newspapers during their day. Bowles was editor of the *Springfield Daily Republican* from 1844 to 1878 and, had he not died at the age of 52, may have risen to a more prominent position on the national stage. He received a long overdue treatment in Stephen Weisner's *Embattled Editor: The Life of Samuel Bowles* (1986). Dana began his career at the *New York Tribune* under Greeley and immediately showed his flair by retaining Karl Marx as a European correspondent. From 1868 to 1897 Dana edited the *New York Sun,* turning it into the "newspaperman's newspaper." A highly literate man, Dana translated Goethe and other authors from the German and wrote first-class travel books. Scholars working on Dana would find Candace Stone's *Dana and the Sun* (1938) the best starting point.

Immigrant editors, apart from Joseph Pulitzer, have received relatively little scholarly attention. Carl Schurz, a German immigrant who became a leading voice for reform in the United States and eventually a senator from Missouri, was also active in journalism, editing the *St. Louis Westliche Post* from 1867 to 1906 and the *New York Evening Post* from 1881 to 1883. Hans L.

Trefousse's *Carl Schurz, a Biography* (1982) is a solid recent study. Karl Heinzen, publisher of the liberal *Der Pioneer*, is the subject of Carl Wittke's *Against the Current: The Life of Karl Heinzen* (1945), an interesting study of another German journalist in America. Emory Lindquist's *An Immigrant's American Odyssey: A Biography of Ernst Skarstadt* (1974) covers that Swedish-American newspaperman's career. The huge majority of 19th-century immigrant journalists have, unfortunately, remained nameless in studies of that century's newspapering. Much work could be done in this field to rectify that neglect—a group portrait, for instance, of the editors and publishers of the nation's most important ethnic newspapers.

Journalism in the 19th century was predominantly a man's profession, and hence most women's contributions in the field are discussed later in the section on the 20th century. Some women pioneers in journalism did, however, rise to prominence in the 19th century. These include Margaret Fuller, a writer rather than editor and publisher who, like so many journalistic luminaries of the century, received her start under the tutelage of Horace Greeley at the *Tribune*. Her career is covered by Madeleine B. Stern's *The Life of Margaret Fuller* (1942), Bell Gale Chevigny's *The Woman and the Myth: Margaret Fuller's Life and Writings* (1976) and Arthur W. Brown's *Margaret Fuller* (1964). Fuller's own memoirs, published in 1852, provide valuable insights into the journalistic world of that time. Her letters, which evidence the wider cultural circles in which she moved, are being edited by Robert N. Hudspeth, three volumes having appeared to date. Victoria C. Woodhull, an early feminist who with her sister, Tennessee Chaflin, published the scandal sheet *Woodhull and Chaflin's Weekly*, is discussed in M. M. Marberry's *Vicky: A Biography of Victoria Woodhull* (1967) and Johanna Johnston's *Mrs. Satan: The Incredible Saga of Victoria C. Woodhull* (1967).

The last quarter of the 19th century witnessed the rise of the great press barons Scripps, Pulitzer and Hearst. The difference between these three publishers and the three titan publishers of a generation or two earlier, Greeley, Bryant and Bowles, illustrates a striking change in American journalism—its leading publishers became more businessmen and less philosophers of public policy. Apart from Scripps, these new publishers wrote little; they were more absorbed in managing a large-scale publishing enterprise. Henceforth the roles of editor and publisher would be more sharply distinct.

A study examining this transformation in the role of the publisher, perhaps with special regard to the careers of the six mentioned above, would be most interesting.

Scripps, founder of the nation's first great newspaper chain, did do some writing about himself. *Damned Old Crank: A Self-Portrait of E. W. Scripps, Drawn from His Unpublished Writings*, edited by Charles P. McCabe (1951), and *I Protest: Selected Disquisitions of E. W. Scripps*, edited by Oliver H. Knight (1966), are two attempts to bring together some of this eccentric man's disparate writings about himself. Negley D. Cochran's *E. W. Scripps* (1933) is a solid but dated biography of him.

Pulitzer got his start in newspapering under Carl Schurz and went on to publish the *St. Louis Post-Dispatch* and *New York World*. W. A. Swanberg's *Pulitzer* (1967) is the best biography of him while George Juergen's *Joseph Pulitzer and the New York World* (1966) mixes biography and newspaper history. Homer W. King's *Pulitzer's Prize Editor: A Biography of John A. Cockerill, 1845–1896* (1965) tells the story of Pulitzer's chief editorial assistant. The three most balanced treatments of William Randolph Hearst are W. A. Swanberg's *Citizen Hearst: A Biography of William Randolph Hearst* (1961), John Tebbel's *The Life and Good Times of William Randolph Hearst* (1952), and Oliver Carlson and Ernest Sutherland Bates' *Hearst, Lord of San Simeon* (1936).

There are many avenues of study open to researchers of 19th-century editors and publishers. As Richard Schwarzlose has pointed out, the New York publishers of the early penny press have received extensive attention while their counterparts in Boston, Philadelphia and Baltimore have been ignored. We also lack a good study of Benjamin Day and the Beach family of the *New York Sun*. One might also examine more closely the symbiosis between politics and journalism in the early 19th century. We know, for instance, that James Watson Webb was a Henry Clay supporter while James Gordon Bennett was a Jacksonian. But what were the underlying reasons for this and what impact did such political-journalistic marriages have on both the politicians and on the newspapers? One might look at the attitude of the penny press toward abolition. Another topic for study would be the changing attitudes of American editors and publishers toward Europe. When, for instance, did they begin to look less to Europe as the center of culture and begin to advance an indigenous American culture? One could also explore the so called middle-class ideology expounded by 19th-century editors and publishers. What sort of treatment did they give broad societal concepts like utilitarianism or egalitarianism?

19TH-CENTURY REPORTERS, CORRESPONDENTS AND ESSAYISTS

COMPARED WITH the 19th-century's editors and publishers, its writers have received relatively scant attention. In terms of intellect and personality, the century's correspondents in general pale beside its editors and publishers, though there certainly were some outstanding writers. As Schwarzlose notes, correspondents and reporters in the early part of the century were often former journeyman printers, not particularly well educated or inclined to deep thought about the problems of their day. Unlike reporters and correspondents of today who sometimes attain celebrity-like status, those of the early 19th century hardly saw themselves as literary figures, an attitude evidenced by the fact that few reporters of the period bothered to write down their reflections or memoirs. The Civil War appears to have been a turning point in this regard, for it was the experience of that cataclysmic event that prompted many reporters to begin to record their afterthoughts. Secondly, around mid-century most major papers had permanent correspondents stationed in Washington, and from their perch near the center of the nation's politics many of these correspondents began to take an interest in recording their own observations on the political scene in the capital.

There are a few books on antebellum reporters. The career of Bayard Taylor, who wrote essays and travel sketches for the *Tribune*, is discussed in Paul C. Weymuth's *Bayard Taylor* (1973). Another *Tribune* essayist, Charles T. Congdon, recounts his career from 1857 to 1882 in *Reminiscences of a Journalist* (1880). Joseph Tinker Buckingham's two-volume *Personal Memoirs and Recollections of Editorial Life* (1852) and his *Specimens of Newspaper Literature: With Personal Memoirs, Anecdotes, and Reminiscences* (1850) are valuable sources. *The Memoirs of Henry Villard, Journalist and Financier* (2 vols., 1904) also contain many insights into mid-19th century newspapering.

John Bigelow, a frequent contributor to the *Evening Post*, describes his career in his five-volume *Retrospections of an Active Life* (1909-1913). Margaret Clapp's excellent *Forgotten First Citizen, John Bigelow* (1947) provides a historical assessment of this journalist. Other studies of or writings about antebellum reporters, correspondents and essayists include Broadus Mitchell's *Frederick Law Olmsted, A Critic of the Old South* (1924), Horace Elisha Scudder's *James Russell Lowell: A Biography* (1901), Claire McGlinchee's concise analysis of Lowell's writings in *James Russell Lowell* (1967), and William S. Robinson's *"Warrington" Pen Portraits: A Collection of Personal and Political Reminiscences from 1848 to 1876 from the Writings of William S. Robinson*, edited by his wife in 1877.

The Civil War was the decisive historical event of the American 19th century, and it goes without saying that its impression upon the journalists of the time was profound. In addition to reportage for their newspapers, many reporters felt compelled to capture their eyewitness experiences in memoir form. Junius Henri Browne of the *New York Tribune* describes his wartime experiences, which included capture by the Confederates at Vicksburg, in *Four Years in Secessia: Adventures Within and Beyond the Union Lines* (1865). Albert D. Richard, another *Tribune* writer, whose ordeal mirrored that of Browne (capture and imprisonment at Vicksburg), recorded his experiences in *The Secret Service, the Field, the Dungeon, and the Escape* (1865). Other fascinating wartime memoirs include Thomas W. Knox's *Camp-fire and Cotton Field: Southern Adventure in Time of War* (1865); George Townshend's 1866 book *Campaigns of a Non-Combatant*, reissued as *Rustics in Rebellion: A Yankee Reporter on the Road to Richmond, 1861–1865* (1950); Franc B. Wilkie's *Pen and Powder* (1888) and *Personal Reminiscences of Thirty-five Years of Journalism* (1891); Sylvanus Cadwallader's *Three Years with Grant as Recalled by War Correspondent Sylvanus Cadwallader* (1955); and *Boston Journal* correspondent Charles Carleton Coffin's *Four Years of Fighting* (1866), Bernard Weisberger's *Reporters for the Union* (1953) and Emmet Crozier's *Yankee Reporters, 1861–65* (1956) examine war coverage from the Northern perspective. Little work has yet been done on Southern reporters.

Nineteenth-century Washington was hardly a political mecca on the order of London or Paris. A lazy, almost small-town capital of a country that prided itself on small government, Washington does not appear to have been a terribly vibrant place during the first century of our nationhood. Not until the 1850s did the correspondents stationed there begin to take an interest in recording their memoirs. Lawrence A. Gobright, the Associated Press' bureau chief in the capital at mid-century, produced in 1869 his *Recollection of Men and Things at Washington During the Third of a Century*. Benjamin Perley, the *Boston Journal's* correspondent in Washington, published his fascinating *Perley's Reminiscences of Sixty Years in the Nation's Metropolis* in 1886. Jane Grey Swisshelm, a feminist abolitionist, and editor and publisher, who was briefly the *New York Tribune's* Washington correspondent, wrote hundreds of letters that are revealing about that time and place. They were edited in 1934 by Arthur J. Larsen under the title *Crusader and Feminist: Letters of Jane Grey Swisshelm, 1858–1865*. See also Swisshelm's memoir, *Half a Century* (1880). Mary Clemmer Ames, who reported for the *Evening Post* and the *New York Independent*, describes her experiences in *Ten Years in Washington: Life and Scenes in the National Capital as a Woman Sees Them* (1873).

The mid-19th century also saw a boom in the number of American correspondents stationed abroad, particularly in the European capitals. Before the Civil War the top newspapers typically had a man of letters, often a European, stationed in London or Paris or Rome, who wrote occasional pieces and sent them by ship. Karl Marx was one such correspondent. But the advent of the trans-Atlantic cable in 1866 ushered in a new era: American newspapers could receive same-day reports on European events, and thus the number of correspondents assigned to Europe boomed. George W. Smalley, assigned to the *Tribune's* London desk in 1867, recounts the trials and tribulations of an American reporter abroad in his *Anglo-American Memories* (1910-12). Harold Frederic, the *New York Times'* correspondent in London, has his story told by Thomas F. O'Donnell and Hoyt C. Franchere in *Harold Frederic* (1961). Two foreign correspondents who roved outside of Europe were Julius Chambers, whose *News Hunting on Three Continents* (1921) records his adventures, and Henry Stanley, who tracked his story into the heart of Africa in search of Dr. David Livingston. Stanley's wife, Dorothy, edited his *Autobiography* in 1906. Ian Anstruther's *Dr. Livingston, I Presume?* (1957) and Richard Hall's *Stanley: An Adventurer Explored* (1975) are solid biographies of him.

A hallmark of 19th-century journalism was the many witty humorists who wrote under pen names, Mark Twain being the most renowned of these. Twain wrote for the *Virginia City* (Nevada) *Territorial Enterprise* and several California newspapers from 1862 to 1869, before a brief stint as editor of the *Buffalo Express*. Albert Bigelow Paine's three-volume *Mark Twain: A Biography, The Personal and Literary Life of Samuel Langhorne Clemens* (1912) is the best biography of him. Ivan Benson's *Mark Twain's Western Years* (1938) and Paul Fatout's *Mark Twain in Virginia City* (1964) give extensive coverage to his early newspaper days. Justin Kaplan's *Mr. Clemens and Mark Twain* is also an excellent biography.

Artemus Ward, pen name of Charles Farrar Brown, was another humorist of this ilk. Don C. Seitz's *Artemus Ward: A Biography and Bibliography* (1919) and James C. Austin's *Artemus Ward* (1964) assess his career. Another 19th-century newspaper wit was David Ross Locke, also known as Petroleum V. Nasby, who wrote for the *Toledo Blade*. Locke edited some of his own writings in *The Nasby Letters, Being the Original Nasby Letters as Written During His Lifetime* (1893). Biographies include John M. Harrison's *The Man Who Made Nasby, David Ross Locke* (1969) and James C. Austin's *Petroleum V. Nasby* (1965). Nellie Bly, pen name for Elizabeth Cochrane, was well known in her day for her exploits as a *New York World* reporter, most notably for her globe-circling journeys. Mignon Rittenhouse's *The Amazing Nellie Bly* recounts some of her adventures.

Just as the late 19th century saw the rise of a new type of publisher, personified by Scripps, Pulitzer and Hearst, so, too, it witnessed the appearance of a new type of writer, the specialist—the satirist, the reformer, the muckraker, the humorist—whose uniquely personal brand of journalism was held out to the public as a special attraction, an inducement to purchase one paper rather than another. Whereas early 19th-century reporters, correspondents and essayists were relatively unknown to the wider public, their late 19th-century counterparts were considered crucial selling points for a newspaper; there developed what we today know as the columnist. Ambrose Bierce, columnist for the *San Francisco Examiner* and the *New York Journal* from 1887 to 1906, was one of the greatest wordsmiths America has ever produced. His life is covered by Casey McWilliams' *Ambrose Bierce, A Biography* (1929), Richard O'Connor's *Ambrose Bierce, A Biography* (1967) and M. E. Grenader's *Ambrose Bierce* (1971). Lovelorn columnist Dorothy Dix is discussed in *Dear Dorothy Dix: The Story of a Compassionate Woman* (1952) by Harnett T. Kane and Ella Bentley Arthur. The famous muckraker Lincoln Steffens did much of his best writing for *McClure's* magazine. He was, however, also a newspaperman, and his massive *Autobiography* (1931), as well as fine biographies by Justin Kaplan and Patrick F. Palermo, provides insights into American journalism around the turn of the century. Theodore Dreiser's *A Book About Myself* (1922) describes his early days as a newspaper journalist, as does Philip L. Gerber's concise biography *Theodore Dreiser* (1963). George Ade and Finley Peter Dunne were two Midwestern columnists whose gentle humor was a major selling point for their respective papers. Lee Coyle's *George Ade* (1964), Charles Fanning's *Finley Peter Dunne and Mr. Dooley: The Chicago Years* (1978), and Grace Eckley's *Finley Peter Dunne* (1981) are fine studies of their lives.

Dale L. Walker recently resurrected the relatively unknown Januarius McGahan in his excellent book *Januarius McGahan, The Life and Campaigns of an American War Correspondent* (1988). Though the title might lead one to think immediately of the Civil War, it was the Russo-Turk Wars in Eastern Europe that McGahan covered. Walker unearthed a great fund of source material, immersed himself in McGahan's historical and cultural milieu, and then spun out his tale in vivid and lucid prose, making this book far more interesting than many works on more renowned journalists.

Where excellent source material exists, such as that on McGahan, more biographies of individual reporters, correspondents and essayists may be warranted, but what is really needed are studies that would synthesize some of the more detailed work on individual journalists. For instance, more interesting than another biography of another 19th-century Washington correspondent would be a work that would pull together several individual stories and paint a picture of what the whole journalistic scene in the nation's capital was like in the 19th century. Similarly, one might try to consolidate the studies of individual Civil War correspondents into a work that would broadly convey the world and the experiences of the American Civil War reporter. Louis M. Starr's *Bohemian Brigade: The Civil War Newsmen in Action* (1954) is a good step in this direction but probably not the last word on the subject. Joyce Milton's *The Yellow Kids: Foreign Correspondents in the Heyday of Yellow Journalism* (1989), which treats the correspondents in Cuba during the Spanish-American War—Stephen Crane, Richard Harding Davis and James Creelman, among others—is another interesting monograph of this ilk. Likewise for the 19th-century columnist, what is needed is not another biography of an individual columnist but a work that would synthesize newspaper columnists' experiences and draw some generalizations about them: What accounts for their rise? What did they have in common?

20TH-CENTURY EDITORS AND PUBLISHERS

CONSIDERABLY LESS HAS BEEN WRITTEN about 20th-century editors and publishers than about 20th-century reporters, correspondents and essayists—quite the reverse of the 19th-century case. This is due primarily to a development that we have already observed in discussing Scripps, Pulitzer and Hearst: Publishers, and to a lesser extent editors, have become business moguls, and the role of philosophizing about society and politics has devolved into the hands of the reporters, correspondents and essayists. Whereas the 18th and 19th centuries were an era of newspaper foundings and journalistic individualism, the 20th century has been an era of consolidation and chain ownership. This change is evident in perusing the literature on our century's editors and publishers.

No publisher of the early 20th century was more single-minded in his application of business methods to journalism than Frank Munsey. Beginning with his purchase of the New York *Daily News* in 1901, Munsey amassed a stable of newspapers based in New York, Philadelphia and Baltimore, sometimes ruthlessly merging flourishing papers out of a concern for the bottom line. George Britt's *Forty Years - Forty Millions: The Career of Frank A. Munsey* (1935) tells his story. A contemporary of Munsey, Frank Gannett launched the newspaper chain that is now the nation's largest. A revealing portrait of Gannett's longtime chief executive officer, Allen H. Neuharth, is Neuharth's own *Confessions of an S.O.B.* (1989). Samuel T. Williamson's *Imprint of a Publisher: The Story of Frank Gannett and His Independent Newspapers* (1948) assesses Gannett's career. S. I. Newhouse owned several small New York papers in the 1920s and '30s and during the next three decades expanded to become owner of the *New Orleans Times-*

Picayune, New Orleans States-Item, Cleveland Plain Dealer, and an immensely rich man. Richard H. Meeker's *Newspaperman: S. I. Newhouse and the Business of News* (1983) is a solid treatment of Newhouse's life. John A. Lent's *Newhouse, Newspapers, Nuisances* (1966) is strongest on the business aspects of Newhouse's empire. *The Copley Press,* published in 1953 by the Copley Press, features a short biography of the chain's founder, Colonel Ira Copley, and chapters discussing each of the 15 dailies in the Copley chain.

Gardner Cowles, owner of several Des Moines and Minneapolis newspapers, and his longtime friend and editor Harvey Ingham are discussed in George S. Mills' *Harvey Ingham and Gardner Cowles, Sr.: Things Don't Just Happen* (1977). In addition to owning the *New York Times* from 1896 to 1935, Adolph S. Ochs published papers in Chattanooga and Philadelphia. Gerald W. Johnson's *An Honorable Titan: A Biographical Study of Adolph S. Ochs* (1946) analyzes his life. Ochs' successor at the *Times*, Arthur Hays Sulzberger, has yet to have his biography written. Frank Knox, another newspaper group owner, led an active life of letters and public service. His life is recounted in Norman Beasley's *Frank Knox: American* (1936), a biography that does not cover the last important years of Knox's life. An important and useful biography of John S. Knight, *Knight: A Publisher in the Tumultuous Century,* by Charles Whited, appeared in 1988. Some major group owners of the 20th century, such as C. K. McClatchy and Herman Ridder, have not yet had their biographies written.

The lives of some great publishing families are closely intermingled with those of their flagship newspapers. Robert R. McCormick, longtime publisher of the *Chicago Tribune,* is discussed in Frank Waldrop's *McCormick of Chicago* (1966), in John Tebbel's *An American Dynasty* (1947) and in Joseph Gies' *The Colonel of Chicago* (1979). Gwen Morgan and Arthur Veysey's *Poor Little Rich Boy* (1985) is the most recent work on McCormick. Eugene Meyer, a Wall Street banker by profession, broke into publishing in his late 50s when he bought the *Washington Post.* Merlo J. Pusey recounts his story in *Eugene Meyer* (1974). The life and career of Meyer's daughter, the *Post's* present publisher, is covered in *Katharine the Great: Katharine Graham and the Washington Post* (1979) by Deborah David. Cissy Patterson, granddaughter of Joseph Medill and cousin of Robert R. McCormick, was also an influential figure in Washington as publisher of the *Washington Times-Herald.* Three good biographies of her are Paul F. Healy's *Cissy: The Biography of Eleanor "Cissy" Patterson* (1966), Alice Albright Hoge's *Cissy Patterson* (1941), and Ralph G. Martin's *Cissy: The Extraordinary Life of Eleanor Medill Patterson* (1979). Dorothy Schiff, who owned the *New York Post* from 1939 to 1977, is discussed in Jeffrey Potter's *Men, Money and Magic: The Story of Dorothy Schiff* (1976). The Annenberg family made its fortune in the Philadelphia newspaper world, publishing the *Inquirer* and the *Daily News*. Gaeton Fonzi's *Annenberg: A Biography of Power* (1970) is a critical treatment of Walter Annenberg's career. John Cooney's *The Annenbergs* (1982) deals with both father and son. The Field family made its fortune in retail but spent it on the *Chicago Sun*. Stephen Becker's *Marshall Field III: A Biography* (1964) discusses the founder of the *Sun* in 1941. The Otises and Chandlers of the *Los Angeles Times* are discussed in the books about that paper cited earlier (see p. 3). A most insightful short piece on them is Joan Didion's article in the February 26, 1990 issue of the *New Yorker*, which masterfully blends biography, newspaper history and city history.

Ralph McGill, "the conscience of the South," who had a long illustrious career as editor and publisher of the *Atlanta Constitution*, wrote an autobiography entitled *The South and the Southerner* (1963). Biographies of McGill include Calvin McLeod Logue's *Ralph McGill, Editor and Publisher* (1969) and Harold H. Martin's *Ralph McGill, Reporter* (1973). Southern editors and publishers like McGill were an instrumental force in liberalizing the region and pushing for equal treatment for blacks. Hodding Carter, editor of the *Greenville* (Mississippi) *Delta Democrat-Times*, has written several books on this subject, the best of which are *Where Main Street Meets the River* (1953) and *First Person Rural* (1963). John T. Kneebone's excellent study *Southern Liberal Journalists and the Issue of Race, 1920–1944* (1985) probes the evolving attitudes toward black civil rights in the South through the lives of five journalists: McGill, Carter, Virginius Dabney of the *Richmond Times-Dispatch*, George Milton of the *Chattanooga News* and Gerald W. Johnson of the *Baltimore Evening Sun*. Kneebone's approach is precisely the sort that students of American newspapering need to take in the future: It deals with a group of journalists rather than focusing on one journalist in isolation, and it is issue-oriented, pulling out important themes rather than showering the reader with anecdotes and details from its subjects' lives.

Voices of Change: Southern Pulitzer Prize Winners takes a similar tack: Maurine H. Beasley and Richard R. Harlow compiled interviews with Southern journalists like W. Horace Carter, Caro Brown and Ira Harkey Jr. centering around the common theme of their writings on civil rights. Harkey, owner of the *Pascagoula Chronicle*, recounts his life story in *The Smell of Burning Crosses: An Autobiography of a Mississippi Newspaperman* (1967). A similar story is that of Clayton Rand, who as owner of the *Neshoba Democrat* in Philadelphia, Mississippi, castigated the Ku Klux Klan and the oppression of blacks in the South. Rand published his autobiography *Ink on My Hands* in 1940. Gary Huey's fine study *Rebel with a Cause: P. D. East, Southern Liberalism and the Civil Rights Movement, 1953–1971* (1985) assesses the career of the editor and publisher of the *Petal* (Mississippi) *Paper*. East tells his own story in the *Magnolia Jungle: The Life, Times and Education of a Southern Editor* (1960). Charles W. Eagles' *Jonathan Daniels and Race Relations: The Evolution of a Southern Liberal* (1982) traces the development of the Raleigh newspaperman. Other works focusing on a uniquely Southern brand of journalism are *A Lifetime on Deadline: Self-Portrait of a Southern Journalist* (1976) by George W. Healy, a former editor of the *New Orleans Times-Picayune*; and Daniel Webster Hollis' interesting study *An Alabama Newspaper Tradition: Grover C. Hall and the Hall Family* (1983) deals with Southern journalism from a familial perspective.

The 20th century has been one of both triumph and disappointment for the black press. While many black newspapers were founded, their lifespans have tended to be short, and no standard nationwide black paper has emerged. William Monroe Trotter, founder in 1901 of Boston's black paper, the *Boston Guardian*, is described in Stephen R. Fox's *Guardian of Boston, William Monroe Trotter* (1970). Roi Ottley's *The Lonely Warrior: The Life and Times of Robert S. Abbott* (1955) tells the story of the founder of the *Chicago Defender*, one of the nation's longest-living black dailies. Robert L. Vann, editor for three decades of the black *Pittsburgh Courier*, is discussed in Andrew Buni's *Robert L. Vann of the Pittsburgh Courier: Politics and Black Journalism* (1974). P. B. Young ran one of the most respected black papers, the *Norfolk Journal and Guide*, for 52 years. Henry Lewis Suggs traces his career in *P. B. Young, Newspaperman: Race, Politics and Journalism in the New South* (1988). Several important black editors and publishers, notably Ida B. Wells-Barnett of Memphis' *Free Speech* and John H. Murphy Sr. of Baltimore's *Afro-American*, have yet to have their biographies written. Enoch P. Water of the *Chicago Defender* had his *American Diary: A Personal History of the Black Press* published in 1987, an interesting book unfortunately marred by frequent spelling and grammatical errors.

Perhaps out of personal biases, scholars have been disinclined to tackle tabloid papers and their journalists as a subject. Simon M. Bessie's *Jazz Journalism* (1938) is an early and intelligent account of the rise of the tabloids. The truly eccentric Bernarr Macfadden, publisher of the *New York Daily Graphic*, had his life covered in *Dumbbells and Carrot Strips: The Story of Bernarr Macfadden* (1953), authored by his wife, Mary Macfadden, and Emile Gauvreau. Gauvreau, editor of Hearst's New York tabloid, the *Mirror*, also recounts his own life in *My Last Million Readers* (1941). Gene Fowler's 1933 work *Timber Line* treats the life of Harry H. Tammen and Fred G. Bonfils, publishers of the garish *Denver Post*. Joseph Medill Patterson, creator of the highly sensational *Illustrated Daily News*, at one time the largest circulating paper in the country, has not yet found a biographer. Nor is there a satisfactory work on today's biggest tabloid mogul, Rupert Murdoch. A fine study of early sensational papers is John D. Stevens' *Sensationalism in the New York Press* (1991).

The rising importance of the press organizations, particularly the Associated Press and United Press International, was one of the most important phenomena in 20th-century American newspapering. Kent Cooper, longtime head of the AP, published a rather self-congratulatory memoir, *Kent Cooper and the Associated Press: An Autobiography*, in 1959. Hugh Baillie, chief of UPI from 1935 to 1955, recounts his experiences in *High Tension: The Recollections of Hugh Baillie* (1959). No solid biographies of Baillie or Cooper exist. Biographical material about news service staffers is found in Oliver Gramling's *AP: The Story of News* (1940), and Joe Alex Morris' *Deadline Every Minute: The Story of the United Press* (1957). Richard Schwarzlose has recently produced a definitive history of cooperative newsgathering from the 1830s to 1920 in his two-volume study, *The Nation's Newsbrokers* (1989).

Several good books have been written on our century's most influential editors. O. K. Bovard, editor of the *St. Louis Post-Dispatch* from 1908-1938, is covered in James W. Markham's excellent biography *Bovard of the*

Post-Dispatch (1954). Joseph Frazier has written on Louisville's *Henry Watterson, Reconstructed Rebel* (1956). Oliver Carlson produced a good but now dated study of *Arthur Brisbane: A Candid Biography* (1937). Carr Van Anda's career is covered by Barnett Fine in *A Giant of the Press: Carr Van Anda* (1933). Willis J. Abbott, editor of the *Christian Science Monitor*, wrote an interesting autobiography, *Watching the World Go By*, in 1933. Ralph Ingersoll edited *PM*, a rather experimental New York City paper that tried to forgo advertising but ultimately failed. Roy Hoopes tells his story in *Ralph Ingersoll: A Biography* (1985). Vermont Royster, longtime editor of the *Wall Street Journal*, recounts his experiences in *My Own, My Country's Time: A Journalist's Journey* (1983), a first-rate memoir, as does another *Wall Street Journal* editor, William F. Kerby, in *A Proud Profession* (1981). Turner Catledge's *My Life and The Times* (1971) is a candid and valuable account of his days at the *New York Times*. Joseph Goulden's recent *Fit to Print: A. M. Rosenthal and His Times* (1988) is a rather gossipy affair, certainly not the final word on Rosenthal. The career of Herbert Bayard Swope, chief editor of the *New York World* and pioneer of the op-ed page is assessed in two fine biographies: E. J. Kahn's *The World of Swope* (1965) and Alfred Allan Lewis' *Man of the World, Herbert Bayard Swope: A Charmed Life of Pulitzer Prizes, Poker and Politics* (1978). Basil "Stuffy" Walters, editor at the *Chicago Daily News*, was another innovator, particularly in the area of typology. Raymond Moscowitz describes his career in *Stuffy: The Life of Newspaper Pioneer Basil "Stuffy" Walters* (1982). *New Guardians of the Press: Selected Profiles of America's Women Newspaper Editors* (1983), edited by Judith G. Clabes, contains short profiles of contemporary women editors.

William Allen White's reputation continues to grow. Editor and owner of the *Emporia Daily and Weekly Gazette* from 1895 to 1944, White came to embody small-town, middle-class American attitudes and values. The vast amount of material he left behind has made him a favorite subject of biographers. White wrote extensively, and his letters, edited by Walter Johnson and published in 1947, reveal much about American life in the first half of this century. Frank C. Clough, Everett Rich, David Hinshaw, Walter Johnson and John DeWitt McKee have all provided serviceable biographies of this important figure. Sally Foreman Griffith's *Home Town News: William Allen White and the Emporia Gazette* (1989) provides an excellent example of the great potential of journalism history. The book is less a biography than a reconstruction of small-town American life seen through the life of White. In *White and the Emporia Gazette* Griffith sees all the facets of local life—psychological, social, cultural, economic and political—woven together. This fine book, along with Joan Didion's *New Yorker* article on the Otises and Chandlers, ought to point scholars of newspapers away from narrow studies of individuals and individual papers and into the more fascinating terrain of synthetic cultural history.

20TH-CENTURY REPORTERS, CORRESPONDENTS AND ESSAYISTS

A HUGE NUMBER OF BOOKS by and on 20th-century reporters, correspondents and essayists exist. Whereas 19th-century reporters slogged away in relative obscurity while their editors and publishers cut profiles as public figures, 20th-century reporters have, to a large extent, seized the limelight from their bosses in the top-story offices. Conscious of their increasing celebrity, many major journalists have felt compelled to record their experiences, observations and opinions in book form. These books by reporters, correspondents and essayists tend to fall into three broad categories: books which focus on the reporter's particular assignment, books which are very autobiographical and personal in tone, and books which raise wider issues on journalism and news reporting. In addition to these books by journalists, this section will take a look at some biographies of 20th-century reporters, correspondents and essayists.

The United States burst to the forefront of the international stage during the 20th century, and its journalists were instrumental in shaping the public's attitude toward America's new world role. George Creel, for instance, a Kansas City and Denver essayist, came to Washington during World War I and became director of President Wilson's Committee of Public Information. During the first years of World War II, Creel's was an influential voice urging American intervention. In *Rebel at Large: Recollections of Fifty Crowded Years* (1947), he tells his own story. An expanded stable of American correspondents abroad also sought to educate the public on the European conflict of

1914. Webb Miller's *I Found No Peace* (1936) is a wise memoir by a longtime UP writer. Paul Scott Mowrer and his brother Edgar Ansel Mowrer both served the *Chicago Daily News* in Paris during the war. Paul Mowrer's *The House of Europe* (1945) is an account of European politics from a very personal perspective. Edgar's autobiography, *Triumph and Turmoil: A Personal History of Our Times*, was published in 1968 and was supplemented by the memoirs of his wife, Lilian, entitled *Journalist's Wife*. John Hohenberg's *Foreign Correspondence: The Great Reporters and Their Times* (1964) is a comprehensive look at that brand of newspaper writing.

Though better remembered as a novelist, Jack London, during a brief stint with Hearst's news organization, also brought home to Americans the international events of the first decades of our century. His daughter, Joan London, provides an account of his life in *Jack London and His Times: An Unconventional Biography* (1939). Other biographies include Richard O'Connor's *Jack London: A Biography* (1964) and Earle Labor's *Jack London* (1974). *Bullets, Bottles and Gardenias* (1935) by Timothy G. Turner deals with London's reportage on the Mexican revolution of 1910 to 1916. Another novelist whose start came as a newspaperman was Ernest Hemingway, who wrote on both domestic and foreign events. Numerous biographies of him exist, Earl H. Rovit's *Ernest Hemingway* (1963) being perhaps the best concise introduction. Charles A. Fenton's *The Apprenticeship of Ernest Hemingway* (1954) and Robert O. Stephens' *Hemingway's Nonfiction: The Public Voice* (1968) pay close attention to his journalistic endeavors, as does the first volume of Peter Griffin's biography *Along with Youth: Hemingway, the Early Years*, published in 1985.

On the home front, no voice was more clarion on matters of foreign policy than that of the "Sage of Baltimore," H. L. Mencken. Mencken made no effort to hide his pro-German sentiments—a source of irritation to his superiors at the *Baltimore Evening Sun*, particularly after the sinking of the Lusitania. In 1917 Mencken left for Europe and covered life in the trenches and reported on the generals in Berlin. Of course, it would be misleading to pigeonhole this great debunker as a writer on foreign affairs. Mencken's interests were universal, and in the journalistic world he was probably without peer during the 1920s. Of the many biographies of this journalist-editor-critic-author-satirist-philologist, Carl Bode's *Mencken* (1969) is perhaps the best. Mencken's own *Newspaper Days*, originally published in 1941, reissued in

1987, covers his years with the Baltimore press. Two volumes of letters, one edited by Guy J. Forgue in 1961, the other by Carl Bode in 1977, and Mencken's recently published *Diaries* offer many valuable insights.

There are many fine memoirs by journalists who covered Europe after the First World War. George Seldes, foreign correspondent for the *Chicago Tribune* from 1917 to 1928, recollected his experiences in his 1953 book *Tell the Truth and Run*. Marguerite Harrison, stationed in Russia immediately after the revolution, tells her story in *There's Always Tomorrow: The Story of a Checkered Life* (1935). Perhaps our greatest correspondent on Soviet matters was Walter Duranty of the *New York Times*. During a time of ideological fervor, Duranty maintained a remarkable clarity and evenness of tone, for which he was awarded the Pulitzer Prize in 1932. In *I Write as I Please* (1935), he summed up his experiences in Russia from 1921 to 1935. A more critical biography of Duranty's career, S. J. Taylor's *Stalin's Apologist: Walter Duranty, the New York Times' Man in Moscow*, was published in 1990. William L. Shirer wrote on German matters for a variety of news organizations during the 1930s and '40s. His *Berlin Diary: The Journal of a Foreign Correspondent, 1934–1941* (1941) and *End of a Berlin Diary* (1947) are first rate. His more recent autobiographical work, *20th-Century Journey: A Memoir of a Life and the Times* (1976, 1984), provides his observations on our turbulent century.

William Henry Chamberlain of the *Christian Science Monitor* and Herbert L. Matthews of the *New York Times* were two other premier foreign correspondents of the '20s, '30s and '40s. Chamberlain reflected on his experiences in *The Confessions of an Individualist* (1940). Matthews assessed his career in *The Education of a Correspondent* (1946). Matthews' coverage of Fidel Castro's Cuban revolution caused some stir, an event examined by Jerry W. Knudson in *Herbert L. Matthews and the Cuban Story* (1978). C. L. Sulzberger, nephew of the *New York Times'* publisher and the paper's chief foreign correspondent and foreign affairs columnist around mid-century, produced a lengthy and rather rambling three-volume memoir: *A Long Row of Candles* (1969), *Last of the Giants* (1970) and *An Age of Mediocrity* (1973), which nevertheless contains a great deal of interesting material. Harrison E. Salisbury was another of the *Times'* finest foreign correspondents. He recorded his Russian experiences in *American in Russia* (1955); his famous foray into the North Vietnamese camp in *Behind the Lines, December 23, 1966–January*

7, 1967 (1967); more reflections on the Soviet Union in *A Journey for Our Times: A Memoir* (1983); and most recently his long march with Mao in *The Long March: The Untold Story* (1985).

Will Irwin, reporter for the *San Francisco Chronicle* and the *New York Sun*, a close friend and biographer of Herbert Hoover, was one of our century's most versatile newspapermen. He wrote *The Making of a Reporter* in 1942, six years before his death. Irwin's *The American Newspaper*, which first appeared in *Collier's* in 1911, represents an early penetrating look at our press. Robert V. Hudson's *The Writing Game: A Biography of Will Irwin* (1982) is a solid biography of him. Gene Fowler, a reporter in Hearst's New York organization, wrote two memoirs, *A Solo in Tom-toms* (1946) and *Skyline: A Reporter's Reminiscences of the 1920s* (1961). H. Allen Smith offers a good biography in *The Life and Legend of Gene Fowler* (1977). Ben Hecht, whose career had one foot in the *Chicago Daily News* and the other in vaudeville, had a tremendous literary output. Doug Fetherling's *The Five Lives of Ben Hecht* (1977) examines his frenetic life as do two recent biographical efforts by William MacAdams in 1988 and 1990. Hecht's autobiography, *Child of the Century* (1954), is an excellent read. Hecht's frequent collaborator on screenplays, also associated with the "Chicago Literary Renaissance" of the 1920s and 1930s, was Charles MacArthur. Hecht wrote the biography of his friend and collaborator in *Charlie: The Improbable Life and Times of Charles MacArthur* (1957), which discusses MacArthur's days as a reporter for the *Chicago Examiner* and the *Chicago Tribune*.

At the *New York Times*, Meyer Berger was the star reporter from the 1920s through the 1950s. Berger wrote his memoirs, *The Eight Million: Journal of a New York Correspondent*, in 1942, 17 years before his death. Later he produced his history of the *Times* (see above, p. 4). A short biographical treatment of him is needed. Alexander Dana Noyes, the influential financial editor at the *Times*, wrote *The Market Place: Reminiscences of a Financial Editor* in 1938. At the *Washington Post*, Chalmers M. Roberts was the top reporter. Like Berger for the *Times*, it fell upon him to produce a history of the paper (see above, p. 3). Roberts wrote his autobiography, *First Rough Draft: A Journalist's Journal of Our Times*, which was published in 1973. Another important *Post* writer was Maxine Cheshire, whose memoirs, *Maxine Cheshire, Reporter*, written with John Greenya, appeared in 1978.

BOOKS ABOUT JOURNALISTS

Several important Washington correspondents have produced memoirs or autobiographies. Charles G. Ross, longtime *St. Louis Post-Dispatch* correspondent and later press secretary for President Truman, is discussed in Ronald T. Farrar's excellent biography *The Reluctant Servant: The Story of Charles G. Ross* (1969). Raymond Clapper, who wrote for UPI, the Scripps-Howard papers and the *Washington Post*, was an integral part of the Washington press scene in the '20s, '30s and '40s until his tragic death in the Pacific war theater in 1941. No good biography of him exists. Drew Pearson published a witty collection of essays on Washington society and politics in *Washington Merry-Go-Round* (1931). The crusty Arthur Krock was practically an institution in Washington, where he served the *New York Times* from 1927 to 1966. His *Memoirs: Sixty Years on the Firing Line* (1968) recounts his journalistic experiences. Associated Press reporter Bess Furman covered the White House during the war years and tells her story in *Washington By-Line: The Personal History of a Newspaperwoman*. Merriman Smith took the White House beat for UPI from 1941 to 1970 and offers many interesting insights in *Thank You, Mr. President: A White House Notebook* (1946). Joseph and Stewart Alsop's *The Reporter's Trade* (1958) is a well-written book on Washington reporting, including a large selection of their own work as columnists. William L. Rivers has produced a penetrating study of the Washington press scene in *The Opinionmakers* (1965). Hedrick Smith's recent *The Power Game: How Washington Works* (1988) is an excellent insider's look at the political machinations in our nation's capital.

Beginning with Marion Marzolf's *Up From the Footnotes* (1977), scholars have begun to examine the neglected topic of women in journalism. In 1983, Madelon Golden Schilpp and Sharon M. Murphy produced *Great Women of the Press*. Barbara Belford's *Brilliant Bylines: A Biographical Anthology of Notable Newspaperwomen in America* (1986) contains 24 biographical sketches of women journalists from the 1800s and 1900s. Most recently, Julia Edward's *Women of the World: The Great Foreign Correspondents* (1988) has appeared. Such works are valuable not only for introducing us to previously overlooked women journalists, but also for the comparative perspective they provide by dealing with groups of journalists. Such group biographies, however, which exclude newspapermen, are predicated on the notion that the newspaperwoman's experience is markedly different from that of her male counterparts. One might assume, on the contrary, that Bess Furman's career, to pick an example, had more in common with Arthur Krock's and that her story might be more fruitfully juxtaposed with his than with those of her fellow female journalist Margaret Fuller, who was writing a century before.

Twentieth-century America's mania for sports is reflected in the appearance of major sports journalists. Ring Lardner, sports columnist for the *Chicago Tribune* and later the Bell Syndicate, whose witty style placed him in the tradition of George Ade, Finley Peter Dunne and Mark Twain, has gone down as the dean of American sports journalists. His life has been covered in three good biographies: Donald Elder's *Ring Lardner, A Biography* (1956), Jonathan Yardley's *Ring: A Biography of Ring Lardner* (1977) and Walton R. Patrick's *Ring Lardner* (1963). Ed Sullivan, who went on to host a massively successful television show, began as a sports columnist. Michael David Harris discusses his media odyssey in *Always on Sunday, Ed Sullivan: An Inside View* (1968). Heywood Broun was another columnist whose first newspaper stint was as a sports writer. Always a clever wordsmith, Broun went on to write a syndicated column, "It Seems to Me," in which he offered his ideas on a wide range of topics. Dale Kramer's *Heywood Broun: A Biographical Portrait* (1949) and Richard O'Connor's *Heywood Broun: A Biography* (1975) assess his career.

Along with H. L. Mencken, Walter Lippmann was probably this century's most important newspaper writer. Lippmann's career in newspapers began in 1922 when he was brought aboard Hearst's *New York World*. When that paper failed in 1931, he moved to the *New York Herald Tribune*, where his column "Today and Tomorrow" came to be the most respected in the country. By the time he ceased to write the column in 1971, Lippmann was lionized as the greatest thinker on public policy in the American 20th century. Ronald Steel's *Walter Lippmann and the American Century* (1980) is a definitive biography of him. Also worthwhile is the collection of essays on Lippmann in *Walter Lippmann and His Times* (1959), edited by Marquis Childs and James Reston, and, particularly for journalists, John Luskin's *Lippmann, Liberty and the Press* (1972).

New York City in the 20th century was a magnet for fast-talking, facile-writing columnists who served as humorists and critics of art and culture on the city's papers. Irvin S. Cobb, the *New York World* humorist, produced two autobiographical books, *Stickfuls: Compositions of a Newspaper Minion* (1923) and *Exit Laughing* (1941). Fred G. Neumann wrote his life story, *Irvin S. Cobb: His Life and Achievements*, in 1934. The humor columnist Don Marquis is portrayed in Lynn Lee's *Don Marquis* (1981). Alexander Woollcott, New York's premier drama critic early in the century, is the subject of Wayne Chatterton's *Alexander Woollcott* (1978). Dorothy Thompson, who began as a foreign correspondent for the *Philadelphia Public Ledger* and the *New York Post* and later became a syndicated columnist, is discussed in Marion K. Sanders' excellent biography, *Dorothy Thompson, A Legend in Her Time* (1973). Westbrook Pegler, whose column "Fair Enough" appeared in the Scripps-Howard papers and later the Hearst papers, is the subject of Oliver Pilat's *Pegler, Angry Man of the Press* (1973) and Finis Farr's *Fair Enough: The Life of Westbrook Pegler* (1975). Walter Winchell, longtime gossip columnist and man-about-town, is portrayed in Ed Weiner's *Let's Go to Press: A Biography of Walter Winchell* (1955). More recently, Russell Baker's *The Good Times* (1989) offers a puckish glimpse at the world of American journalism in the 20th century. By far the best and most comprehensive treatment of American journalists and their role in newspapers is Loren Ghiglione's *The American Journalist* (1990).

CARTOONISTS AND PHOTOGRAPHERS

THERE ARE A HANDFUL OF GOOD BOOKS on newspaper cartoonists and newspaper photographers, or photojournalists as they are sometimes called. Cartoons, especially political cartoons, have of course an older pedigree than newspaper photos. American newspapers have been carrying cartoons since colonial times. Photographs first began to appear in American newspapers in 1880. Stephen Hess and Milton Kaplan's *The Ungentlemanly Art, A History of American Political Cartoons* (1968) is a good introduction to the subject. Also valuable are William Murrell's *A History of American Graphic Humor,* (2 vols.) (reprinted in 1967) and Allan Nevins and Frank Weitenkampf's *A Century of Political Cartoons, Caricature in the United States from 1800–1900* (1944). Another useful introduction is *Comic Art in*

America: A Social History of the Funnies, the Political Cartoon, Magazine Humor, Sporting Cartoons and Animated Cartoons (1959) by Stephen Becker. Mary and Gordon Campbell's *The Pen, Not the Sword, A Collection of Great Political Cartoons from 1879 to 1898* (1971), by focusing on a particular time period, is able to go into greater depth, and offers insights on the political world of the time, especially municipal government and international relations. The cartoons are mostly drawn from *Puck* and *Judge*.

Thomas Nast probably has the greatest reputation of any political cartoonist. He is remembered above all for his biting caricatures in *Harper's* magazine attacking Tammany corruption. Albert Bigelow Paine wrote an early and still first-rate book on Nast, *Thomas Nast, His Period and His Pictures* (1904). Two fine and more recent biographies of Nast are Morton Keller's *The Art and Politics of Thomas Nast* (1968) and J. Chal Vinson's *Thomas Nast, Political Cartoonist* (1967). Joseph Keppler's lithographic cartoons for *Puck* are beautifully reproduced and accompanied by biographical and historical text in Richard Samuel West's recent *Satire on Stone: The Political Cartoons of Joseph Keppler* (1988). Homer Davenport, an important cartoonist for Hearst's *San Francisco Examiner* and *New York Evening Journal,* gained international fame at the turn of the century and became one of the country's highest paid journalists. Mickey Hickman chronicles his life in *Homer: The Country Boy* (1986).

Joseph North has written on the socialist cartoonist Robert Minor in *Robert Minor, Artist and Crusader, An Informal Biography* (1956). Art Young was another cartoonist of socialist leanings. He produced an autobiography, *Art Young, His Life and Times* (1939), which was edited by John Nicholas Beffel. John T. McCutcheon, a cartoonist for the *Chicago Tribune,* offered his recollections in *Drawn from Memory* (1950), and the *New York Times* cartoonist S. J. Wolfe recorded his memories in *Here I Am* (1941). Walt MacDougall's *This Is the Life!* (1926) is another memoir by a renowned cartoonist. John Chase's *Today's Cartoon* (1962) also presents brief biographical sketches of the cartoonists of the time.

Although there is little biographical work on recent and contemporary cartoonists, many of the better known cartoonists, such as Herb Block, Pat Oliphant, Bill Maudlin and Garry Trudeau, have published collections of their work. Garry Trudeau's work bridges the political cartoon and the traditional comic strip. Bill Blackbeard and Martin Williams have collected an anthology of comics, *The Smithsonian Collection of Newspaper Comics* (1977). There are two anthologies of Pulitzer Prize-winning pieces: Dick Spencer III's *Pulitzer Prize Cartoons: The Men and Their Masterpieces* (1951) and Gerald W. Johnson's *The Lines Are Drawn: American Life since the First World War as Reflected in Pulitzer Prize Cartoons* (1958), which also provides some useful commentary. See also Thomas Craven's *Cartoon Cavalcade* (1943). A monumental recent study is David Kunzle's *The History of the Comic Strip* (1990).

There is little work specifically on news photography or news photojournalism. Many of the books on this subject are texts designed to teach photojournalism rather than scholarly books about photojournalism. The best work of this sort is Gerald D. Hurley and Angus MacDougall's *Visual Impact in Print: How to Make Pictures Communicate, A Guide for the Photographer, the Editor, the Designer* (1971). Marianne Fulton's recent *Eyes of Time, Photojournalism in America* is an excellent collection of photographs preceded by a thoughtful introduction. *Scoop, Scandal and Strife, A Study of Photography in Newspapers* (1971) edited by Ken Baynes, is also a fine introduction to the topic. Sheryle and John Leekley have compiled *Moments, the Pulitzer Prize Photographs* (1978), which contains fine reproductions of the prize-winning photographs, but offers little commentary.

There is certainly room for a more scholarly and historical approach to studying photojournalism. Photographers, for instance, arguably did more to alter modern notions about war than did prose journalists. The first photographs ever to appear were shot during the Crimean War, 1853–55. They disenchanted British public opinion, which led to reduced support for the war, and ultimately influenced the course of British foreign policy during the war. During the First World War, some photos of trench warfare were so horrific that most governments censored them. The strong impact of news photographs during the Vietnam War would alone provide material enough for a serious study. This is but one example of avenues for further study of news photography.

CONCLUSION

As this essay has tried to show, the history of American newspapering is a field ripe for consolidation. Many studies of individual papers and individual journalists stock our shelves, and rather than adding to their number scholars should look to producing more synthetic works, which would pose more overarching questions about the American press and deal with journalists and papers in groups rather than in isolation. A large percentage of the works cited in this essay were written by journalists themselves. Perhaps one reason that non-journalism scholars—historians, political scientists, sociologists—have been slow to recognize the font of information available in our nation's newspaper collections is that newspapering does not neatly fit into any of these traditional disciplines. But as I have tried to suggest, this is too limited a view of newspapers' scholarly utility, for the papers and journalists need not only be the *subject* of study but can also be the *means*. That is to say, newspapers provide a unique portal through which a scholar can get a glimpse of society as a whole. They yield not only the information printed in black and white but, if one reads between the lines, they tell about the underlying assumptions and values of the society that produces and reads them. Thus newspapers should not be viewed only as a source of material for journalism history, but as material for urban history, religious history, ethnic history and much more. In this sense, we have only begun to explore the great warehouse of Americana that is our newspaper collections.

AN INVENTORY
OF MAJOR NEWSPAPER ARCHIVES

LIBRARY OF CONGRESS

James Madison Building
101 Independence Ave, S.E.
Washington, D.C. 20540
(202) 707-5000

THE LIBRARY OF CONGRESS is the largest repository of newspapers in the country, maintaining a collection of roughly 2,450,000 issues (both U.S. and foreign newspapers). The number of U.S. issues only is approximately 900,000. A total of 38,591 newspaper titles are preserved in the collection. Of these, 14,350 are U.S. newspaper titles, ranging in date from the late-17th century to the present day. The Library currently receives 363 U.S. newspapers that it retains on a permanent basis and an additional 124 U.S. newspapers that are retained on a current basis only.

Massachusetts, New York, Pennsylvania, Maryland, Illinois and Ohio are the states best represented in the collection. The Library has a particularly strong black newspaper collection. Its collection of 18th-century newspapers is the most extensive in the nation. The Library has also emphasized collecting newspaper titles from the original 13 states for the 19th and 20th centuries. The collection has long consecutive runs for many of the nation's major newspapers: the *New York Times*, *Washington Post*, *Evening Star* (D.C.), *New York Herald Tribune*, *Chicago Tribune*, *Baltimore Sun*, *New York Journal American*, *Savannah Morning News*, *San Francisco Chronicle* and *Los Angeles Herald*.

The Library of Congress holds numerous papers of special historical significance. For instance, it has originals or reprints of *The Boston Gazette* and *Country Journal* of March 12, 1770, covering the Boston Massacre; of *The Boston News-Letter* of April 24, 1704, the first issue of the first regularly published American newspaper; of *Gazette of the United States, New York*, of May

2, 1789, covering Washington's inauguration; of Isaiah Thomas' *The Massachusetts Spy* of May 3, 1775; of the February 11, 1723, *New England Courant*, the first publication under the imprint of Benjamin Franklin, to name a few. The Library also has a special collection of U.S. bicentennial newspapers, printed between July 1 and 6, 1976.

All of the Library's holdings are still intact enough to read. About 85 percent of its titles have been microfilmed. Many of the Library's most recent issues of major American newspapers are available on the Datatimes and Vu/Text databases. Also, the Library is spearheading the U.S. Newspaper Project, which will enter bibliographical and holdings records into the OCLC/CONSER database, making about a quarter of a million newspaper titles available to researchers throughout the nation. The Library also has the nation's largest collection of newspaper indexes and other reference materials to aid researchers. The Library is open to the public seven days a week. The newspaper collection operates a closed-shelf system.

THE STATE HISTORICAL SOCIETY OF WISCONSIN
816 State Street
Madison, Wisconsin 53706
(608) 262-3266

THE STATE HISTORICAL SOCIETY OF WISCONSIN has the second largest collection of newspapers in the United States. It is a national collection spanning the period from the 17th century to the present that has been developed to serve the needs of researchers not only in Wisconsin but throughout the world. The collection totals approximately 14.5 million issues, including foreign newspapers. The Society holds roughly 15,000 titles, 12,000 of which are post-Civil War titles; 3,000, pre-Civil War. Currently about 500 titles are being preserved. These include about 320 Wisconsin titles, 20 of which are received on microfilm; 25 national dailies received on microfilm; and the rest black, native American, ethnic and other newspapers.

With more than 7,500 titles, Wisconsin is the state most strongly represented in the collection. Other prominent states are Illinois, New York,

Michigan, Massachusetts, Minnesota, Ohio, Pennsylvania and Virginia. The Society possesses the largest collection of colonial and early American newspapers west of the Appalachians, the largest collection of labor newspapers in the nation, and the most extensive holdings of underground or alternative newspapers in the country. Other areas of concentration are 19th-century religious newspapers, black newspapers, ethnic newspapers, military, radical/reform, abolitionist, women's and native American newspapers.

Among the rarities in the newspaper collection are the first black and native American newspapers, as well as the first Dutch-, Spanish-, Norwegian- and Czech-language newspapers published in the United States. Some of the longest consecutive runs in the collection include the *Milwaukee Sentinel* (1844-present), *Chicago Tribune* (1849-present), *Detroit Free Press* (1837-1940), the Madison, Wisconsin, *Wisconsin State Journal* (1852-present), and the *Washington Post* (1877-present). The Society also has many commemorative and special newspaper issues: V-E and V-J Day issues (in military newspapers such as *Stars and Stripes*); Lincoln assassination issues (*New York Herald, New York Tribune, National Intelligencer*); Kennedy assassination issues; Washington death issues; the first public printing of the Constitution (in the *Pennsylvania Packet*); 25th, 50th, 75th, and centennial anniversary editions of the *New York Times*; 50th and centennial editions of the *Milwaukee Sentinel*; original Benjamin Franklin issues of the *Pennsylvania Gazette*; and the first newspaper published in Wisconsin, the *Green Bay Intelligencer*, in December 1833.

The Society's collection consists of 11,340 bound volumes, 95,000 reels of positive and negative microfilm, and 17,168 sheets of microprint. Approximately 85 percent of the newspapers have been microfilmed, 5 percent are on microprint, and the remaining 10 percent are hard copy. The Society microfilms all Wisconsin newspapers as a matter of course. Most of the hard-copy newspapers are still intact enough to read. The Society has been a participant in the U.S. Newspaper Project, and its collection is open to the public. Patrons gain access to the holdings by use of the catalogues in the main reading room. The Society provides interlibrary service for any microfilmed newspapers to libraries throughout the United States and abroad.

AMERICAN ANTIQUARIAN SOCIETY

185 Salisbury Street
Worcester, Massachusetts 01609-1634
(508) 755-5221

THE AMERICAN ANTIQUARIAN SOCIETY is the United States' primary repository for early American newspapers. Building on Isaiah Thomas' gift in 1812 of 382 titles in 551 volumes, the Society has accumulated more than 15,000 newspaper titles in 20,000 volumes. The Society has more than 2 million issues on five miles of shelving and adds about 3,000 issues a year to its holdings.

The collection is composed of newspapers from all 50 states and the District of Columbia, the Canadian provinces, the West Indies, Great Britain, Mexico and Latin America. British newspapers are maintained through the Revolutionary War period; newspapers from Latin America and the non-English-speaking Caribbean countries are retained but no longer acquired.

The Society's collection of pre-1821 American newspapers is the world's finest, containing 1,494 titles. The following newspapers are a sample of the Society's holdings for this period: *The Boston News-Letter*, the first continuously published newspaper on this continent; *The Pennsylvania Evening-Post*, printed in Philadelphia and the first attempt at an American daily newspaper; *The New York Weekly Journal*, printed by Peter and Catherine Zenger from 1734 to 1751; and one of the two extant copies of the oft-reprinted *Ulster County Gazette* from Kingston, New York, reporting on George Washington's death. The Society holds the only copy or copies of 118 of these early titles, among them *The Senator* (1814) from Washington, D.C., and the *Herald of Liberty* (1798-1802) from Washington, Pennsylvania. The post-1820 holdings are also among the best in the country. The general cut-off date for collecting at the Society is 1876, although for Western states some newspapers after 1876 are collected.

Not surprisingly, the depth and breadth of newspaper holdings at the Society are greatest for the Eastern United States. These include 1,588 titles for Massachusetts; 1,323 for Pennsylvania; 1,493 for New York; 844 for Ohio; 300 or more each from Georgia, California, Illinois, Indiana, Maine, Michigan, Missouri, New Hampshire, Tennessee and Wisconsin; more than 200 each from Connecticut, Kentucky, Louisiana, Maryland, Mississippi, New Jersey, Rhode Island and Vermont; and more than 100 each for Colorado, Minnesota, Nebraska, North Carolina, South Carolina, Texas, West Virginia and the District of Columbia. The Society has many titles for a few states west of the Mississippi, such as Iowa (446) and Kansas (176), including some long runs.

The Society collects newspapers of special interest groups—religious, temperance, literary and ethnic—German- and French-language newspapers and black newspapers. The Society also has copies of "wallpaper newspapers"—newspapers printed on the back of wallpaper samples because of the paper shortage in the Southern states during the Civil War. The Society has three copies, each on different wallpaper, of the most famous of these newspapers, the *Daily Citizen* from Vicksburg, Mississippi, for July 2 and July 4, 1863.

Because the collections of the Society are shelved in areas closed to the public, researchers gain access to them through the general catalogue, bibliographical tools, and terminals linked to national databases. The Society is a participant in the U.S. Newspaper Project.

NEW YORK HISTORICAL SOCIETY
170 Central Park West
New York, New York 10024-5194
(212) 873-3400

THE NEW YORK HISTORICAL SOCIETY preserves a newspaper collection of roughly 1.5 million issues. It maintains the fourth largest collection of pre-1820 U.S. newspapers. Of the Society's 8,800 newspaper titles, 700 were printed before 1820. Three hundred titles are post-1900, and the majority are from 1820–1900. New York City is well represented in this latter range, but the bulk of the rest of the collection is pre-Civil War.

New York City and state are best represented in the Society's collection. Holdings include consecutive runs of the big New York dailies: the *Evening Post, Tribune, Herald-Tribune, Times, World* and *Sun* on microfilm, and of *The Commercial Advertiser* in hard copy. The Society's collection of the more short-lived New York colonial, revolutionary and federal era newspapers is nearly complete. The Society also preserves an especially large number of pre-Civil War titles for Pennsylvania and Massachusetts.

In addition to its concentration on New York City 18th- and 19th-century newspapers, the Society has especially strong collections of California newspapers from the gold rush era, and of army and navy newspapers of the Civil War. The Society has a sample issue of each newspaper printed in the United States in 1873. Its indexes of New York City newspapers are also unique: for instance, a crude index of the *Evening Post*, 1873–1921; and a card index of the *Sun*, 1913–1920; and *Herald*, 1920–1924. Many commemorative newspapers are interspersed within the collection. The collection also features newspapers covering the 1906 San Francisco earthquake and the New York blizzard of 1888. It has the first issue of the *New York Times.* Also to be seen are Confederate newspapers printed on wallpaper, ledger paper, etc., due to the wartime paper shortage.

Some late-19th- and early-20th-century newspapers are too fragile to handle without damaging. Some 19th-century material is poorly bound and must be handled with care. Only about 5 percent of the titles are on microfilm, but this includes a much larger percentage of issues that are used; the Society insists that patrons use microfilm rather than hard copy when it is available. Small microfilming requests are honored, and the Society will produce copies of master negatives at cost.

The library at the Historical Society is open to all college-age users; non-members of the Society pay an entrance fee to the museum. The library has closed shelves and material is non-circulating. There is a separate card catalogue for newspapers listing them by city of publication. The collection is included in all major bibliographies and in the U. S. Newspaper Project.

NEW YORK PUBLIC LIBRARY

The Annex, 521 W. 43rd Street
New York, New York 10036
(212) 714-8520

THE NEW YORK PUBLIC LIBRARY maintains about 15,000 bound volumes of hard-copy newspapers and approximately 125,000 reels of newspapers on microfilm. The collection has roughly 5,000 titles, of which approximately 400 to 500 are pre-Civil War. New York state is naturally the state best represented in the collection.

The Library has a wide-ranging collection of New York City newspapers. Its collection of ethnic newspapers—Slavic, Jewish and Oriental—is particularly good, as is its collection of black newspapers in the Schomburg Collection located in Harlem. The collection's longest consecutive runs are for the big New York dailies: the *New York Post*, *New York Times*, *New York Herald*, *New York Sun* and *New York Tribune*. The Library also has a collection of newspapers relating to centennial celebrations and histories of American localities in its U.S. History, Local History and Genealogy Division.

The bulk of the collection is on microfilm and the remaining hard-copy titles are microfilmed with some exceptions. Some titles, primarily pre-1870 newspapers, are still in good condition in hard copy. The collection is closed stack. Readers gain access to the holdings by consulting public catalogues in the Annex (where the papers are housed) or in the Central Research Library.

HARVARD UNIVERSITY

Harvard College Library
Cambridge, Massachusetts 02138
(617) 495-2411

HARVARD'S NEWSPAPER HOLDINGS are spread among several major research libraries: Widener Library (the library of the Faculty of Arts and Sciences), Houghton Library (the rare book and manuscript library), Baker Library of the School of Business Administration, the Slichter Industrial Relations Collection of the Littauer Library, the Andover-Harvard Theological Library, and the Schlesinger Library on the History of Women in America. The decentralized nature of the University's newspaper holdings makes it difficult to quantitatively assess the size and scope of the collection.

Widener Library has the largest collection of newspapers in original paper format or on microfilm in Harvard University Library. There is a special newspaper catalogue in the Widener Library Reading Room that lists titles held by Widener and Houghton libraries, originals and microfilms, by state and place of publication. The collection is strongest for Massachusetts newspapers, with substantial holdings for the other New England states and New York. Original issues of colonial newspapers and rare back files of other titles are generally housed in Houghton Library. Widener Library has numerous microfilmed back files, including many major metropolitan newspapers, the Readex Early American Newspapers, significant numbers of black, Jewish and other ethnic newspapers, and a collection of "underground" newspapers of the 1960s and 1970s. Ten newspaper titles for which Widener Library has long consecutive runs are the *San Francisco Examiner* (1865–present), *Los Angeles Times* (1881–present), *Denver Post* (1895–present), *Atlanta Constitution* (1868–present), *Chicago Tribune* (1847–present), Louisville, Kentucky, *Courier-Journal* (1868–present), New Orleans *Times-Picayune* (1837–present), *Baltimore Sun* (1837–present), *Detroit News* (1873–present), and *St. Louis Post-Dispatch* (1874–present).

Hard-copy newspapers held by Widener Library are stored in the New England Deposit Library (located in Boston) and must be requested through the Widener Circulation Division. Most original newspapers are in deteriorating condition and cannot sustain heavy use. The Library replaces original holdings with microfilm as necessary and as funds permit. Whenever a unique or substantial file of a newspaper is identified (and found not to be available on microfilm), the Harvard Library will undertake to make a preservation film. The Library cooperates with the Boston Public Library in the Massachusetts Newspaper Project and makes its holdings of Massachusetts titles available for filming. The Library has also assisted other state projects to ensure that unique titles or issues in the Harvard collections are made available for microfilming. Preservation, access and other questions of policy may vary from library to library.

UNIVERSITY OF WASHINGTON

Suzzallo Library
University of Washington Libraries, FM-25
Seattle, Washington 98195
(206) 543-2553

THE SUZZALLO LIBRARY preserves approximately 2 million newspaper issues in microfilm and hard copy. The collection has about 1,100 U.S. newspaper titles, 150 of them dating from the pre-Civil War era. The vast majority of the collection is post-Civil War, about 950 titles. Each year the library microfilms about 70 newspaper titles: generally 60 American titles, largely from Washington state, and 10 foreign titles.

The states most strongly represented in the collection are Washington and Alaska. Pacific Northwest newspapers in general is the Library's main area of emphasis. Alaska and Yukon gold rush newspapers constitute a particular area of interest. The collection is also strong in labor movement and Seattle newspapers. There is a substantial collection of Filipino-American newspapers (about 50 titles), concentrated particularly in the 1930s and 1940s. The Library has long consecutive runs for several Northwestern newspapers, including *The Oregonian* (Portland), *Seattle Post Intelligencer*, *Spokesman Review* (Spokane) and *Seattle Times*. The Library has two special collections: the Pacific Northwest Collection and a special collection that houses hard-copy issues of anniversary editions of Washington state newspapers.

The collection is in good condition but crowded. Hard-copy issues are, for the most part, still legible. About 95 percent of the permanent collection has been filmed. The Library microfilms select newspaper titles that they want to retain permanently and that are not otherwise available on film. They store master copies of all titles they film themselves. The microfilm collection is open stack. The materials do not circulate, but almost all of the collection can be borrowed through interlibrary loan. Hard-copy holdings of the permanent collection are, for the most part, stored in secured areas and retrieved for users on request. *Pacific Northwest Newspapers on Microfilm at the University of Washington Libraries*, published in 1983, and holdings records on OCLC provide access to off-campus users. The collection is also included in the U.S. Newspaper Project; Washington state records should be incorporated in the national project in 1990.

BOSTON PUBLIC LIBRARY
666 Boylston Street, P.O. Box 286
Boston, Massachusetts 02117
(617) 536-5400

THE BOSTON PUBLIC LIBRARY first opened its newspaper collection in 1895. Since then it has developed into a major newspaper repository, preserving roughly 1,750 American titles. About 800 of these titles are pre-Civil War, 950 of them post-Civil War. Currently the Library is collecting 134 titles.

The Library emphasizes Boston and ethnic newspapers. Massachusetts, New York and Pennsylvania are the states for which the collection is the strongest. Long consecutive runs exist for the *Columbian Centinel, New England Palladium and Commercial Advertiser, Boston Daily Advertiser, Boston Traveler, Boston Post, Boston Evening Transcript, Boston Herald, Boston Daily Journal, Boston Globe,* and (Boston) *Record-American.* The Library has many special collections, dealing with topics such as the assassinations of American presidents, the San Francisco earthquake of 1906, fires at Chicago, Boston and Portland (Maine), the East Coast hurricane of 1938, "Grand Army Encampment" (Boston, 1890 and 1904), Emancipation

Proclamation reports, secession documents, Civil War clippings and Confederate newspapers. The condition of the collection varies from fair to good for newspapers published prior to 1860, to unreadable for some material published in the decades prior to and after the turn of the 20th century. Colonial newspapers are now kept in the rare book room and use is limited by conditions set by the keeper. Older back files under the control of the newspaper room can be used only by permission of the curator of microtexts and newspapers. However, because the Library has actively pursued the preservation of its newspaper holdings over the last 30 years through microfilming programs or the purchase of titles from microform vendors, most of the material requested for use by patrons is in microform in the microtext department and original files seldom need to be consulted.

Newspaper holdings in the microtext department include about 1,400 titles, mostly from Massachusetts, and contain substantial to complete runs of all the major newspapers from Massachusetts towns and cities, and all colonial newspapers available in microform. This material, however, represents less than half of the newspaper titles held by the Library. The Library is the coordinating agency for the Massachusetts Newspaper Program under the U.S. Newspaper Program established through the National Endowment for the Humanities and will eventually hold microfilm files of all Massachusetts newspapers. The number of filmed titles may well reach 3,500.

UNIVERSITY OF TEXAS AT AUSTIN
Eugene C. Barker Texas History Center
SRH 2.109
Austin, Texas 78713-7330
(512) 471-5961

THE EUGENE C. BARKER Texas History Center of the Library of the University of Texas at Austin preserves approximately 15,500 volumes of hard-copy newspapers and more than 12,000 reels of microfilm. The volumes vary as to the number of issues in each. The Barker Center's collection has 3,800 titles, 1,000 of them pre-Civil War, 2,800 post-Civil War. Texas newspapers dominate the collection with 2,125 titles. The other Southern states are also well represented with 858 titles. The collection has long consecutive runs of several important Southern newspapers, such as *Galveston Daily News* (1865–1945), *Houston Post* (1880–1985), *LaGrange Journal* (1880–1985), *New Braunfels Zeitung* (1852–1953), *San Antonio Express* (1868–1984), and the Vicksburg, Mississippi, *Evening Post* (1884–1968). Holdings also include substantial runs of such important antebellum titles as the *Telegraph* and *Texas Register* (1835–1854) and the *Clarksville Northern Standard* (1842–1888).

The collection features microfilm copies of the first newspaper printed in Texas, the *Gaceta de Texas*, printed in Nacogdoches in 1813, as well as hard-copy issues of the *Texas Gazette* (1829–1831), the first newspaper in Stephen F. Austin's colony and the first permanent newspaper in Texas. Other special-interest titles preserved are the Ku Klux Klan's *Pure Democracy* (1922), and the antiprohibitionist *True Blue* (1887), from Waco. There is also a collection of newspapers dealing with the assassination of President Kennedy. Also of note are special newspaper editions dedicated to centennial celebrations of various Texas towns.

The majority of the newspapers in the collection are intact. About 40 percent of the titles are on microfilm. The titles held in hard copy are bound in buckram or housed in acid-free newspaper storage boxes. Twentieth-century unbound titles are sandwiched between two sheets of cardboard for support and wrapped in kraft paper. The Barker Center has applied to the National Endowment for the Humanities for a grant to support the preservation microfilming phase of the Texas Newspapers Project. Some microfilming is done through patron initiation and support.

The Barker Center uses negative master copies to reproduce copies as requested. Patrons use positive service copies. The hard-copy papers are in closed stacks. The microfilms are in an open-stack area.

THE CONNECTICUT HISTORICAL SOCIETY

One Elizabeth Street at Asylum Avenue
Hartford, Connecticut 06105
(203) 236-5621

THE CONNECTICUT HISTORICAL SOCIETY has an estimated 86,800 issues in its newspaper collection. There are about 473 titles in the collection, 251 of them printed before 1866, 266 of them printed after 1866; 27 titles span that division year. Virtually all of the newspaper titles are from Connecticut or relate in some way to Connecticut.

Papers with the most sizable holdings include the *Hartford Courant*, *Hartford Post*, *Hartford Times*, the *Religious Herald* (Hartford), the *Middletown Constitution*, *Middletown Press*, *Sentinel and Witness* (Middletown), and the *Connecticut Centinel* (Norwich). Two areas of special interest are a small collection of Yale University student papers and a sizable collection of amateur and youth papers. There are also miscellaneous papers covering anniversary events (national, state, town) and some special editions covering natural disasters.

The majority of the Society's collection is in fair to good condition and readable. About 15–20 titles are preserved on microfilm. Hard-copy newspapers are stored flat on shelves. Those that are not bound are stored in acid-free folders or boxes. Materials from the collections are microfilmed as requested by other institutions or patrons. The Society also does some preservation microfilming. The newspaper collection is open for public use. Newspapers are stored in closed stacks and must be retrieved by staff.

THE HISTORICAL SOCIETY OF PENNSLYVANIA

1300 Locust Street
Philadelphia, Pennsylvania 19107
(215) 732-6200

THE HISTORICAL SOCIETY OF PENNSYLVANIA maintains a collection of roughly 200,000 hard copy issues and 50,000 microformat issues. The collection has approximately 1800 U.S. newspaper titles of which about 85 percent are pre-Civil War titles. Eighty-seven of the titles are in microformat. During 1989–90, 10 titles from the Society's collection were microfilmed as part of the Pennsylvania Newspaper Project.

The collection is strongest for the states Pennsylvania, New Jersey, New York, Massachusetts and Ohio. The Society's richest materials fall into the colonial period. It has a newspaper for every day that a paper was published in Pennsylvania. There is also a large number of newspapers gathered at the time of the Philadelphia Centennial Exposition and a good collection of army newspapers from the Civil War, World War I and World War II. The Society's longest consecutive runs are for the *Philadelphia Record, Evening Bulletin, North American, Evening Telegraph, Public Ledger, National Intelligencer* and *Philadelphia Inquirer.*

The collection's pre-1860 newspapers are generally in good shape, flexible and bright. Papers from the period 1860–70 vary in condition— some with low acid content are in fine shape, others are quite brittle. The papers dating from 1870 to 1975 are usually very brittle and their usage is restricted. Papers printed after 1975 are still generally in good shape.

Approximately 5 percent of the collection is on microfilm and readers are referred to the microfilm collection first. When a newspaper is not available in microfilm and is too brittle to handle, the Society will perform microfilming upon patron request. The hard-copy original newspapers are held in closed stacks. The Society's collection is currently being entered into the OCLC database as part of the Pennsylvania Newspaper Project.

DUKE UNIVERSITY LIBRARY
Perkins Library, Duke University
Durham, North Carolina 27706
(919) 684-2947

THE DUKE UNIVERSITY LIBRARY preserves about 100,000 issues in its newspaper collection. The newspapers are housed in acid-free boxes. Many of the collection's North Carolina newspapers have been microfilmed, and through the U.S. Newspaper Project in North Carolina unfilmed North Carolina papers are likely to be microfilmed in the coming years.

Duke's collection has roughly 4,500 titles, about 2,300 of them post-Civil War titles, about 2,200 from the pre-Civil War period. North and South Carolina, Virginia and Massachusetts are the states most strongly represented in Duke's collection. Scholars of the American South would be likely to find useful material among the newspaper holdings. The newspapers for which Duke has the longest consecutive runs are the *Boston Evening*

Transcript, *Des Moines Register*, *Portland* (Maine) *Daily Press*, the *Daily National Intelligencer* (Washington, D.C.), and the *Richmond Enquirer*.

About 50 to 60 percent of the collection's hard-copy papers are also available on microfilm, but this represents only about 20 percent of the titles in Duke's collection. Duke films local newspapers as a matter of course. The library also microfilms on demand for its patrons. Its pre-Civil War papers are in good condition; most post-Civil War papers are brittle but intact, with a few exceptions. The collection has open stacks for post-1870 newspapers and closed stacks for pre-1870 newspapers.

UNIVERSITY OF ILLINOIS AT URBANA-CHAMPAIGN
University Library, 1408 W. Gregory Drive
Urbana, Illinois 61801
(217) 333-1509

THE UNIVERSITY OF ILLINOIS LIBRARY maintains a newspaper collection of 11,289 bound or wrapped volumes of hard-copy newspapers and 79,470 reels of microfilmed newspapers. (This includes foreign newspapers.) Each volume or reel contains 10 to 100 issues. The collection preserves 1,863 U.S. newspaper titles plus 807 underground titles. The holdings concentrate on the late 19th and 20th centuries, but many important back files extend into the early 19th century, and some back to the early 1700s.

Illinois, New York, California and Massachusetts are the states best represented in the University's collection, along with Washington, D.C. Areas of special interest within Illinois' collection are black newspapers, college dailies, underground press and labor and socialist newspapers. Holdings include, for instance, Chicago's *Bilalian News*, from 1961; University of Illinois' *Black Rap*, 1969–71; Oakland's *Black Panther*, 1968–80; Berkeley's (California) *Berkeley Barb*, 1965–80; Denver's *Big Mama Rag*, 1983–84; Chicago's *Broad Ax*, 1897–1927; New York's *Daily Plebeian*, 1842–45; and New York's *Militant*, from 1937. Holdings of newspapers from counties in the Upper Mississippi Valley are particularly extensive.

About 95 percent of the collection is on microfilm. The library has little funding for microfilming but does microfilm newspapers from

Champaign County that are not commercially filmed. The collection is closed stack.

THE BALCH INSTITUTE FOR ETHNIC STUDIES

18 South Seventh Street
Philadelphia, Pennsylvania 19106
(215) 925-8090

THE BALCH INSTITUTE FOR ETHNIC STUDIES in Philadelphia is devoted to furthering scholarship on immigration to the United States and on ethnic groups in America. Its entire collection of 450 titles is composed of ethnic press publications. Twelve of these titles fall into the pre-Civil War period; the rest are post-Civil War newspapers. New York and Pennsylvania are the states most strongly represented in the Balch Institute's collection.

The Institute has long consecutive runs of such papers as the *Philadelphia Tageblatt, New Jersey Freie Zeitung, Philadelphia Gazette Democrat, Dziennik Zwiakowy, Pacific Citizen, Jewish Exponent, Zgoda* and *Slovensky Sokol.* One area of special interest is the Institute's collection of Japanese-American relocation camp newspapers. The library also has the business records of a number of immigrant newspapers, including *Atlantis* (Greek, New York City), *Gwiazda* (Polish, Philadelphia), *Nord Amerika* (German, Philadelphia), and *Polish American Journal* (Scranton).

Of the collection's 450 titles (representing about 65 percent of the total issues), 275 have been microfilmed. Newspapers are microfilmed on a priority basis when funds are available. The public can gain access to the collection through the OCLC database catalogue and through in-house catalogues.

CHICAGO PUBLIC LIBRARY

Newspapers and Periodicals, 400 N. Franklin
Chicago, Illinois 60607
(312) 738-7600

THE CHICAGO PUBLIC LIBRARY preserves more than 500,000 issues in its newspaper collection, this figure excluding newspapers in the Library's special collections. The vast majority of the Library's 323 titles are post-Civil War newspapers. The Library has only eight pre-Civil War titles, along with many titles in its Early American Newspaper Collection. Illinois is the state most strongly represented in the general collection with 58 titles. Other states that figure prominently in the collection are New York and California, along with the District of Columbia.

In addition to its special collection of early American newspapers, the Chicago Public Library has several other special collections of interest. These are a special collection on the history of Chicago newspapers; extensive holdings of foreign language newspapers from Chicago, 1890–1945; and an underground newspaper collection. The Library also has collections covering the Abraham Lincoln assassination; the *Daily Columbian*, May–October 1893, a newspaper covering the World's Columbia Exposition; and a John F. Kennedy Memorial Collection.

More than 95 percent of the Library's holdings are on microfilm. Many of the hard-copy issues of these microfilmed newspapers have been sold. A large portion of the hard-copy papers preserved by the Library are in poor condition but are generally readable. These issues are gradually being filmed. The Library has no microfilming facilities of its own. Microfilmed newspapers are available in open stacks.

CATHOLIC UNIVERSITY OF AMERICA

Mullin Library, 620 Michigan Avenue, N.E.
Washington, D.C. 20064
(202) 319-5060

CATHOLIC UNIVERSITY preserves a small but well-focused newspaper collection in its Mullen Library. Most of its 162 titles are Catholic newspapers, making the collection a primary font of material for scholars of Catholics and Catholicism in America. Forty-five of these 162 titles are pre-Civil War newspapers, while 117 fall into the postwar period. New York, Massachusetts, Indiana and Maryland are the states best represented in Catholic University's holdings, along with the District of Columbia.

The collection preserves long consecutive runs of Catholic newspapers such as Davenport, Iowa's *Catholic Messenger* (1893–present), Cleveland's *Catholic Universe Bulletin* (1874–present), Baltimore's *Catholic Mirror* (1850–1901, 1903–1908), Boston's *The Pilot* (1829–present), and San Diego's *Tidings* (1895–present). There are also substantial holdings of the *Brooklyn Tablet*, the *Catholic Advocate* (Bardstown, Kentucky), the *Catholic Telegraph Register* (Cincinnati), and the *Catholic Worker* (New York).

Catholic University attempts to obtain microfilm of the Catholic newspapers that it receives and preserves. The majority of the collection is on microfilm, although the Library does not have facilities for doing its own microfilming. Apart from papers preserved in special collections, the newspaper collection is open shelf.

KANSAS STATE HISTORICAL SOCIETY

120 W. Tenth Street
Topeka, Kansas 66612-1291
(913) 296-3251

THE KANSAS STATE HISTORICAL SOCIETY is the largest Plains-state newspaper repository. It houses approximately 12,435 titles, the vast majority of which are post-Civil War newspapers. An estimated 10 to 15 percent of the titles are pre-Civil War. Currently, the Society subscribes to and preserves 367 titles.

The collection is naturally strong on Kansas newspapers. Newspapers for which it has long consecutive runs include the *Topeka Capital Journal* (1879-present), *Lawrence Journal World* (1854–present), *Leavenworth Times* (1858-present), and the *Kansas City Star* (1880–present). The Society's newspaper collection has numerous issues touching on aspects of Plains-states history, such as cattle drives, foundings of towns and settlements, and the Pony Express.

About 65 percent of the collection is on microfilm, and the Society has a project underway to film the remaining 35 percent. The collection is closed stack. A detailed guide has been prepared for the microfilmed portion of the collection. Patrons use a card catalogue to locate hard-copy papers.

THE WESTERN RESERVE HISTORICAL SOCIETY
10825 East Boulevard
Cleveland, Ohio 44106
(216) 721-5722

THE WESTERN RESERVE HISTORICAL SOCIETY in Cleveland has a newspaper collection of roughly 250,000 issues. The collection holds approximately 3,600 titles, 25 percent of them pre-Civil War, 75 percent post-Civil War. Ohio is the state best represented in the collection.

The Society has particularly emphasized Civil War ethnic newspapers and ethnic abolitionist newspapers in amassing its collection. The holdings include long consecutive runs for *The Cleveland Plain Dealer*, *The Cleveland Leader*, *The Cleveland Press*, *Cleveland News* and *Cleveland Herald*. Other areas of special interest for which the Society has substantial holdings include the Lincoln and Garfield assassinations.

Most of the collection's newspapers are still readable. Only about 10 percent have been microfilmed. The Society will microfilm for a fee upon patron request; otherwise microfilming proceeds as funds become available. Patrons gain access to the collection through "check cards" in the library. The collection is closed stack.

OREGON HISTORICAL SOCIETY

1230 S. W. Park Avenue
Portland, Oregon 97205
(503) 222-1741

THE OREGON HISTORICAL SOCIETY preserves about 475 newspaper titles, most of which have been microfilmed. About 40 of these titles are pre-Civil War newspapers, the rest are post-bellum.

The Society's collection is strongest for the state of Oregon. Scholars interested in the history of Oregon, of Portland, the Pacific Northwest and the overland journeys would most likely find valuable material in the Society's newspaper collection. The newspapers for which the Society holds the longest consecutive runs are *The Oregonian* (Portland), *Oregon Statesman-Journal* (Salem), *Eugene Register-Guard*, *The Daily Astorian* (Astoria, Oregon), *Medford Mail Tribune*, *The Bulletin* (Bend, Oregon), and *East Oregonian* (Pendleton, Oregon).

The Society's newspaper collection is open to the public and is closed shelf.

THE UNIVERSITY OF MINNESOTA

309 19th Avenue South
Minneapolis, Minnesota 55455-0414
(612) 626-2227

THE LIBRARY OF THE UNIVERSITY OF MINNESOTA has 320 newspaper titles in its collection. Of these, 107 are pre-Civil War and 213 are post-Civil War titles. Currently the Library preserves 21 titles. The collection is particularly strong in newspapers from Midwestern states.

The Library has several collections of papers that are of special interest, such as *Happy Days* (1933–42), the weekly newspaper of the Civilian Conservation Corps; an underground newspaper collection covering the years 1961-85; Japanese internment camp newspapers, 1942–45; American Indian newspapers, 1970–73; and the Inter-Ocean Illustrated Supplement of Chicago, June-December, 1892, an example of the first color printing on a rotary newspaper press in America. The newspapers for which the Library has the longest consecutive runs are the *Minnesota Star-Tribune*, *St. Paul Pioneer Press*, *Chicago Tribune*, *Atlanta Constitution*, *St. Louis Post-Dispatch* and the *Times-Picayune*.

The collection also has a number of commemorative issues, for instance, the *Jackson* (Miss.) *Advocate* of November 9, 1963, an Emancipation Proclamation centennial edition; the *New York Atlas*, 1838–50, the oldest Sunday paper published in New York; and the *New York Daily Advertiser* of March-June 1785, the first newspaper to install the steam-driven cylinder press.

The condition of the collection varies. Most papers are sufficiently intact to read. Newspapers that the Library intends to preserve are generally purchased in microfilm. There is no set policy regarding the microfilming of newspapers. The collection is open stack, apart from older hard-copy issues.

THE NEW JERSEY HISTORICAL SOCIETY

230 Broadway
Newark, New Jersey 07104
(201) 483-3939

THE NEW JERSEY HISTORICAL SOCIETY preserves a newspaper collection of about 900 titles. Roughly 100 of these titles are from the pre-Civil War period. The Society has an ongoing microfilming program, which it coordinates through the New Jersey Newspaper Project. The collection emphasizes New Jersey, New York and Pennsylvania. Its most impressive consecutive runs are of the *Elizabeth Daily Journal* (1872–present); the *Newark Daily Advertiser* (1832–1907); and *The Sentinel of Freedom* (1796–1890). It also has a run of the *New Jersey Gazette,* the first continuously printed newspaper in the state, from 1777 to 1786.

Condition of the collection varies from excellent for the pre-1830 period to extremely poor for the acidic modern papers. Most papers in the collection are readable. A newspaper catalog at the Society guides readers to hard copy originals, which are stored in a vault. Papers on microfilm may be obtained in the reading room.

COLLECTIONS AT SELECTED NEWSPAPERS

MOST NEWSPAPERS maintain collections of their own papers as well as clippings, photographs and negatives, etc., pertaining to their own publications. Many newspaper libraries are for in-house use only or restricted public access. Here is a brief list of the holdings at some of the nation's major newspaper houses:

Los Angeles Times: own newspaper on microform, 1881–present, plus photos and negatives.

San Francisco Chronicle: own newspaper on microform, 1865–present, plus clippings, photos and negatives.

The Washington Post: own newspaper on microform, 1877–present, plus clippings and photos.

Chicago Sun-Times: own newspaper on microform, 1875–present, plus clippings, photographs and negatives.

Chicago Tribune: own newspaper on microform, 1847–present, plus clippings and photographs.

Baltimore Sun: own newspaper on microform, 1837–present, plus clippings and photographs.

Boston Globe: own newspaper on microform, 1872–present, plus clippings and photographs.

St. Louis Post Dispatch: own newspaper on microform, 1874–present, plus clippings and photographs.

New York Post: own newspaper on microform, 1801–present, plus clippings.

Cleveland Plain Dealer: own newspaper on microform, 1842–present, plus clippings and photographs.

Philadelphia Bulletin: own newspaper on microform, 1875–present, plus clippings and photographs.

AUTHOR INDEX

AUTHOR INDEX

AUTHOR INDEX

AUTHOR INDEX

AUTHOR INDEX

AUTHOR INDEX

AUTHOR INDEX

SUBJECT INDEX

SUBJECT INDEX

SUBJECT INDEX

SUBJECT INDEX

SUBJECT INDEX